When Your Teen Is Struggling

Real Hope and Practical Help for Parents Today

Mark Gregston

HEARTLIGHT PUBLISHING

LONGVIEW, TEXAS

Cover by Nolan Abney

Editor: Natalie Gillespie

This book contains stories in which the author has changed people's names and some details of their situations to protect their privacy.

Dedication

This book is dedicated to Jan, my wife of 41 years. She has been there

in our work with kids from the beginning…

and continues to desire

God's best for families and teens everywhere.

Acknowledgments

*W*ith special thanks:

To my daughter and son-in-law, Melissa and Blake Nelson, and my son Adam, who I have the pleasure to work alongside at Heartlight. All three have helped make the Heartlight ministry what it is today.

To all the members of the Heartlight Ministries Foundation Board for the willingness to come alongside Jan and me take lessons learned through the years to those who will never darken the doors of Heartlight. Thank you to Bill and Susanne Walsh, Roger and Lori Kemp, George and Livia Dunklin, Jerry and Leanne Heuer, and Alan and Belinda Carter.

To the Board of Directors for Heartlight: your love and participation continues to make Heartlight a place of help and hope for the desperate families who place their children with us. Thank you to Jonathan and Jillian Greifenkamp, John and Amy Hull, Andy and Lisa Deer, and Mike and Carol Barry.

To Pam Mitchell, Ben Weinert, Ryan and Mariah Blalock, Justin Arnold, Sam Sheeley, Amber Horton, and Sarah Robinson for your dedication to the cause of Heartlight.

To all the staff at Heartlight for your commitment to teens and families, and for inviting these people into your lives. It is a joy to serve alongside each of you.

To Michael Ranville and Nolan Abney, Kemp & Company, Wayne Shepherd (my radio co-host), Joe Carlson (the man behind the big red button – a/k/a radio producer), Randy Steele and Doug Kindy of Lucchese Boots, and Satterwhite Log Homes of Longview, Texas.

To my four grandchildren Maile, Macie, Chase, and Carter, who make me laugh and relax, and who constantly remind me of the preciousness of all children.

Contents

Foreword

$\mathcal{I}$ first shook the hand of a young man named Mark Gregston in 1981. He had just stepped onto the campus of our Kanakuk Kamp to introduce himself as the new Young Life leader for our little town of Branson, Missouri. Little did I know what great friends we would become—and the phenomenal impact he would have over the coming years on the lives of thousands of teenage kids. In fact, in all my years of working with kids—seeing 20,000 a year pass through our Kanakuk Kamp programs—I don't know many men who have made a greater impact on the world of struggling teens.

With more than 40 years of experience working with children and parents who find themselves struggling through the teen years, Mark has become a true expert in understanding the unique challenges facing teens and their families. And he understands so well how to advise parents who are navigating those often rough waters of adolescence.

The Heartlight residential program for struggling teens that he and his beautiful wife Jan began thirty years ago is extremely effective. Hundreds of troubled kids have graduated from that program over the years and have become not only successful adults, but also beautiful Christian men and women. I know of no other program like Heartlight. I have had a chance to meet the moms and dads of some of these kids. They are profoundly grateful for Mark and the skills he built into their lives so they could become the parents they so desperately wanted to be.

Mark refuses to pull any punches or sidestep any sticky or difficult situations, as you will quickly find out in the pages of this book. He speaks directly to the issues confronting parents and teens in this day and provides solid biblical and practical help while sharing his own mistakes, hurts, and struggles.

His heart for helping parents and teens will also become evident very quickly as you read this book. You will see that he has spent countless hours in the trenches with thousands of struggling families, committing to remain there until they are able to get on the other side of their struggle.

While most people his age are trying to find ways to slow down and retire, Mark is constantly searching for new and better ways to meet the needs of parents and families. And this book does just that. I can guarantee that if you are wrestling with how to parent your teen or going through a crisis with your child, or if you have a child about to enter those difficult years, this book is for you!

Joe White
President, Kanakuk Kamps
Branson, Missouri

Introduction

The world your kids live in today is a mess. As they move into their teen years, they face unimaginable pressures to turn away from the values you worked so hard to instill in their lives. Their world is different from the one you and I grew up in. And I think we know that, because I hear many parents and grandparents state, "I am glad I don't have to grow up in this culture." Parenting teens during this time requires a different style of parenting than most parents are used to.

Regardless of how good a parent you are, certain forces are at work to send your kids spinning off in directions you could never imagine. Every day when I wake up and read or listen to the news, I feel a sense of shock at what I am seeing and hearing. And that low-voltage jolt, as subtle as it may feel, reminds me that the culture is changing rapidly. That change in culture requires parents to change the way we parent, in order to ensure that the messages we intend to communicate are given in a way that is effective, memorable, and life-changing for our kids.

In more than forty years of working with troubled teens, I have seen parent after parent wonder what in the world happened, or is happening, to their teen. They seem to wake up one morning and discover their teens have completely changed. Loving, kind, and thoughtful kids turn into people they don't even recognize. No wonder many parents are scared and unprepared for the adolescent years ahead.

Perhaps that's the way you feel today.

Sure, you built hedges around your kids. You tried to raise them God's way. You taught them to just say *no*. You prayed together so you would stay together. You did devotions. You attempted to raise godly children in an ungodly world. And you loved them to no end, only to find they reject the very truth and goals you embrace.

You homeschooled, held ceremonies for your boy to become a man, told your girls that true love waits, and took them to church, camps, and mission projects. But what you thought you could keep from happening—and what you hoped would never happen—is not just knocking on your doorstep. No, it opened the door and walked right into your home.

Now what?

First, let me give you a word of hope. You are not alone. Thousands of Christian parents across the country are struggling with their teens. They feel lost and desire to discover ways to counteract the effects of today's teen culture on their children.

Friend, the Christian family is not immune to the negative effects of this world! It is susceptible to what every Christian parent has worked so hard to prevent. Parenting comes with no guarantees,

At some point, you might ask what makes me so knowledgeable and qualified to share my thoughts and comments with you. It's a great question. Here's my answer: I currently live with 60 high school kids. As a matter of fact, I have lived with more than 3,000 kids over the last 40 years. They're struggling teens trying to put it all together who got lost along the way. I did the youth pastor thing for 7 years, was an Area Director for Young Life for 6 years, and lived at the largest Christian sports camp in the country for 7 years. I have built my life and career around kids and spent my time working with their parents. Out of those experiences, I write this book.

I guarantee you can have hope. That's the reason for this book. I also want to reassure you that you can find a way through your kids' difficult teen years. Navigating these waters is going to take some work, but it's worth it. And you should know that getting your children through these difficult times is going to be as much about you as it is about them.

The good news is that you *can* get to the other side of these adolescent years. And if your relationship with your child is broken, you can restore it.

My desire is to unpack for you what I have learned during the years I have worked with troubled teens and their families.

I want to show you how to deal with your teen and give you hope, direction, and insight whether you are in a crisis situation today or you want to prevent such a day in the future.

May God use this book to enlighten, empower, and encourage you in one of the greatest challenges you will ever face—parenting your teen.

CHAPTER ONE

Hope Amidst the Conflict

You probably opened this book because you are at the end of your rope. You are dealing with disappointment in your child. You may feel abandoned by friends and God. You may be in the pit of despair because you're not exactly where you thought you would be as a parent. You might be asking questions like these:

How did I end up in the very place I worked so hard to avoid?

Why is my child so angry? We gave her everything.

How could we do everything right and everything end up so wrong?

Why is my child making the choices he is?

Why does my child hate me? I have done nothing but love her.

How could something so well-intentioned turn out so bad?

Who is this child who woke up this morning?

Why is my family falling apart? We worked so hard to keep it together.

Or you might be feeling and thinking some of these statements:

I am done.

I quit.

I can't do this anymore.

You've got to be kidding me.

I have nothing left to give.

You desperately need something right now—an expectation, trust, wish, something to look forward to. You need hope. Especially when your relationship with your child seems to be falling apart.

Watching your child go through difficult times and cause conflict and disruption in your household is one of the worst tragedies a family can face. It will move you as a parent into thinking things you never thought you would think. When a desire you have for your child (and perhaps for yourself) vanishes, the pain can be indescribable. You are probably ready for anything that will give you even a glimmer of hope. Perhaps you long to hear that you can turn around the crisis at hand.

I pray that in the following pages you will find hope and encouragement, that you will learn how to deal effectively with your struggling child and better prepare for the potentially difficult years ahead.

Reality Check

The process starts with a reality check. That reality check is simply this:

> Every parent struggles.
>
> If you haven't, you will.
>
> If you are struggling now, you can find hope.

I have sat with thousands of parents who, like you, are trying to understand just what is happening to their families. They are confused and distraught by their children's behavior and choices. They want to know what to do, and they want to know if they have any reason to hope for their family's future.

Not long ago I had just such a meeting with a dad. He sat across from me at a conference table, and with tears in his eyes, a broken heart, and desperation in his words, he said, "Mark, just tell me there's hope for my daughter!"

He is not alone. *You* are not alone.

My wife Jan and I began dating in the ninth grade. Our first date was a Led Zeppelin concert. We spent a lot of time going to concerts. I wanted to see the hard rock bands. She wanted to go see plays and musicals. I consented during our junior year of high school and took her to see a play, my first musical production.

If you have ever seen *Fiddler on the Roof*, you will remember Tevye, the father. Tevye struggled with his youngest daughter, Chava, who made some choices against Tevye's will. In the play, Tevye sings a song called the "Chava Ballet Sequence," which he directed to his youngest daughter, his little bird, showing his frustration and despair. I still tear up when I hear this song. The song pictures a father letting go and reflecting on his daughter with great disappointment.

> *Little Bird, Little Chavaleh,*
> *I don't understand what's happening today.*
> *Everything is all a blur…*
> *Gentle and kind and affectionate,*
> *The sweet little bird you were,*
> *Chavaleh, Chavaleh.*[1]

It was the first time I ever cried at a performance. I saw the hurt and disappointment this father had in his daughter. I felt the pain Tevye so eloquently sang about and identified with the line, "Everything is all a blur." After celebrating forty years of marriage (and both of us turning sixty), Jan and I went to New York to see a Broadway show. Guess which one we picked? You got it. *Fiddler on the Roof*. And when Tevye sang about his daughter, I teared up the same way I did forty-five years ago.

It reminded me of this: Hurt and disappointment have been around for a long time. Matter of fact, since the beginning of time. But families are still intact. Family ties can survive the struggle of children for independence. And you know what?

You can survive this period of your child's adolescence, regardless of the feelings or thoughts you're having right now.

Perhaps you have just gone through a difficult time with your child and you are trying to figure out what happened. Or perhaps you are in the midst of confusion right now, and you wonder if you will ever make it to the other side. Maybe you see something coming, and you want to prepare yourself.

Whatever your situation, you need to understand another reality. God has not abandoned you. In all the confusion and darkness, He is still there. In His Word, He promises to turn ashes into beauty, sadness into joy, and mourning into dancing. These are not just phrases of Scripture that reflect His power and show His ability. They are promises of hope for people in dark times to cling to. They are assurances for parents of teens who are struggling through things they never expected.

Could God be absent? Would He be absent? Not on your life.

Hopelessness or Opportunity?

Hopelessness feels like a dark tunnel with no end. But if you add God to the picture, everything changes. Your seemingly hopeless situation can become one of the greatest opportunities for you and your child to connect in ways far beyond anything you ever dreamed possible.

Over and over again, I have seen parents and their struggling teens travel down the road of life together. As the load lightens, they find hope in the darkness. And they learn things about themselves and each other they could not have learned any other way. The same can happen for you.

This dark chasm you're in will not last forever. This time is only one chapter in your life's story. Don't look for a quick fix, and don't expect to find any timetable except God's.

Albert Einstein made a statement that stuck with me, and I apply it to families working through their problems. He said, "The reason for time is so that everything doesn't happen at once."[2]

Your family's healing won't happen at once.
It will be a journey. But you will get to the other side.

To the dad I mentioned earlier who asked if there was hope for his daughter, my answer was yes. And that is my answer to you today too. You can have hope for your relationship with your child. The answer is not going to come on the timetable you think it will. (It won't happen overnight.) It won't look anything like you think it will. (God's plan is always better than anything we can envision.) But someday you will be amazed at how much better your relationship is with your child. (Really. I mean it!)

But you have to act now. Postponing the inevitable only delays the impact of your teen's actions to a later time when consequences are greater and affect a greater number of people. It's like this: I can either deal with the issues now while my child is at home and I have the opportunity to speak truth into his life. Or I can ignore what is before me and allow my child to deal with it later … when she is married, has children, etc. Get my point? The time to deal with problems and crises is now.

Conflict is a precursor to change. The opportunity before you now is not beyond God's reach, nor is it unreachable by you. How you respond will make a difference in the relationship you have with your child. Timeliness will determine the length of time that your child (and you) are in darkness, and set the tone for the quality of relationship you will have with your child once he leaves home.

The Bigger Picture

Whenever I talk with parents of a child who is out of control, they want to know three things:

1. "Why is this happening?"

2. "Why is my child doing this?"

3. "What do I need to do (or be) to help my child?"

These are good questions that need to be asked and answered. But the answers can only come when you begin to understand God's intent and purpose for families.

The reasons why teens struggle are obvious when something goes terribly wrong in their lives—rape, sexual abuse, death, damage from divorce, or other tragedies. But when everything a parent does is well-intentioned and no obvious trauma causes a child to spin out of control, parents naturally wonder why all this is happening. They question their worthiness as parents or believe they are being punished for something.

Parents are not generally prepared to handle the crisis of an out-of-control teen, because they believe their good parenting should have made their children safe from the pitfalls of life all around them. They believe their children will never make any poor choices and subconsciously feel God should protect their children more than other children. Consequently, they haven't developed the skills to handle crises.

A young father approached me in Los Angeles a number of years ago and asked what I thought about a program called *Growing Kids God's Way.* (I actually get asked about this a lot.) This is a good program for most kids. Truth be told, there are a number of great programs and mind-sets just like GKGW. But they did not work for the type of teens I am usually involved with. I shared that I did not really know much about the program but that several of the families who placed kids with us tried this approach. What I found is that when parents are struggling with their kids, they desperately try every program they can get their hands on.

This dad went on to say that if the parents of the kids in our residential program had used this approach, they evidently did a poor job, or they would not have ended up needing that kind of help. As the hair on my neck began to bristle, I told him I would have to disagree with his statement because parents at Heartlight are some of the neatest people I have ever met, and they love their kids well and did everything possible to resolve the issues their children were going through.

He replied, "Well, my kids will never end up there [at Heartlight]. It just won't happen." He obviously believed his parenting style and skills would shield his kids from trauma and keep them from making bad choices. I responded that I hoped he was right, that his kids would never need the services of the Heartlight residential program and he would never have to go through struggles with his children.

His daughter came to live with us four years later.

This father's former arrogant mind-set is the type of thinking that usually gets parents into trouble.

> *Anyone can have a struggling teen, regardless of*
> *how good you are at being parents.*

This understanding will save you a lot of grief, and you just might prevent your child from going down a path no one would want to walk. It's like this: If I really believe my child will never make poor or inappropriate choices, then I will not prepare myself for the unexpected. If and when my child surprisingly does make life-altering choices, my family is not ready for the conflict we thought we worked so hard to avoid. I tell parents all the time to remember what I learned in Boy Scouts at an early age: "Be Prepared."

Parents tell me they won't have problems because they're doing the "right thing" in the life of their child. My response is that it often has nothing to do with what you are doing right. It has everything to do with a culture that is changing the rules of the game.

Parents face the challenge of guiding kids through the various stages of life. The mind-set and skills you possessed during your children's preteen years may have worked well for you. In preadolescence, parents can do no wrong, life is simpler, and kids look up to and depend on you. But as your child ages and enters the changes of adolescence, you also need to change.

Some of the changes for your kids include brain development (from concrete to abstract thinking), hormones that suddenly make romance important, a desire for freedom and independence, development of different social circles, and changes in their learning styles.

To keep up with the kids, parenting styles need to change too. Lecture must move to discussion. Parents need to shift their role from protector to preparer. A parent who never before had to admit wrongdoing might now confess his or her shortcomings. In addition, through experience and failure, parents must begin to learn how to handle the personal and relational difficulties teens experience. All of this can be overwhelming and emotionally draining. Hope could not come at a better time.

Embrace the Journey

Kids live in a confusing world. We must stay the course in loving and preparing our teens and understand they are on a journey to adulthood. We can embrace the journey they are on by learning some new skills, understanding their world, and discerning the hand of God on their lives. As we give them the freedom to experience this journey, we ultimately foster more authentic relationships with them and allow them to grow personally.

American Author Ursula K. Le Guin wrote, "It is good to have an end to journey towards; but it is the journey that matters, in the end."[3] From where you stand, the journey may appear to be going nowhere. But it could be the greatest journey you and your child will ever experience together. It won't look like what you always thought it would, and it probably won't follow the path you dreamed and hoped you would get to walk. But it can come with its own sweet rewards.

This struggle has come to your family for a reason. You are the parent of this child for a reason. The timing is not accidental. You probably do not understand all the reasons for these struggles, but that does not diminish their purpose or the plan behind them. They are part of the journey God has for you and your child. He will use it all. Regardless of how hard the circumstances may be and how devastating the issues are right now, nothing comes to you that has not first passed through God's hands. The hard times come to transform you more into His image, so He can use you in a greater way for His purpose. Rick Warren stated in the opening line of his book *The Purpose-Driven Life*, "It's not about you."[4] This statement helps define God's purpose for our lives.

However, regarding your current family crisis, it might be about you. After all, the fruit doesn't fall far from the tree. Reflect on some hard questions. Is the conflict with your child actually about you? It could be. Is it about your child? I am sure it is. Is it about your family? Absolutely. Is it also about God? You can bet your life on it.

My point is this: The child you brought home from the hospital many years ago with God's thumbprint on his or her life is the same child today. Just because this child is struggling does not mean the Maker or purpose for being created has changed. If this son or daughter was created for a purpose, as Scripture reminds us he or she was, then that purpose is not being sidetracked just because of a few bumps in the road (regardless of how big they might appear). God can use these bumps to transform your child into a vessel He can better use for His purpose, His glory, and your family's ultimate good.

Please don't hear me say that God *caused* all that is happening. That's a completely different discussion. But I promise you this: He is faithful to use whatever is happening in your life and your child's life for good things in the future. Good things are coming; you just may not be able to see them right now. God is leading you in the journey.

When the Israelites wandered in the desert for forty years, trying to make it to the Promised Land, God guided them with a "pillar of cloud" by day and a "pillar of fire" by night. (See Exodus 13.) The Israelites could not see the end. They could not guide themselves out of the dry, parched land. God never let them see past His hand right in front of them. He provided enough for them to get through each day and no more. That way, they had to rely completely on Him to get to the blessings at the end of the journey.

I can tell you from my experience with families that—short of your child or you dying—you will get to the other side of this time. You may not be able to see the happy ending right now, but God will be faithful to guide you today. He can give you hope for the struggle today. If you trust Him. If you rely on Him. And if you purpose to change and grow with your child on the journey. The path you choose to follow will determine the length of time you and your child struggle with darkness and the quality of relationship you share during the struggle.

For most of my life, I felt quietly disgruntled with the people who did not give me what I wanted, who hurt or offended me, or caused pain in my life. As I add more candles to my birthday cakes each year, turn more gray-haired, and become more reflective, I get this overwhelming sense they will all be standing with God when I get to Heaven. God will say, "Mark, I want you to know I used these people in your life to transform you more into My image and to prepare you for your work with those who were struggling."

Here's an example of what I am talking about:

I had a dream a few years ago that changed the way I viewed the struggle I have always had with my dad. For whatever reason, I never quite felt his blessing on what I pursued in my life. Maybe he felt it, but he never quite communicated it in a way that made me feel comfortable in our relationship. As a result, there was always a distance in our relationship, and a quiet anger I experienced in his presence. I think they are my own "daddy issues" of never feeling loved, never being told I was loved, never feeling supported, and always being quietly shunned and tolerated at the same time. As a result, I have held onto a quiet rage present every time I think about my dad.

Back to the dream. I dreamed that I died, went to Heaven, and walked in the gates. Suddenly, I was face-to-face with my heavenly father. Standing next to God Himself was my dad. I cussed at God (although I don't think this is exactly the correct way to meet the Creator of the universe), asking, "What is my blankety-blank father doing here?" I let out all the pent-up anger at my dad I had accumulated through the years of my disappointment. God looked at me, pointed His finger at me, and said, "Mark, I want you to know something. I have been using this man all your life to create in you the person I wanted you to be."

That was it. He didn't say anything else.

He didn't have to.

I awoke and immediately knew God just spoke to me in the dream. That is the only time that's ever happened … it has not happened since. But I knew He was trying to get a message to me that could only be given to me when my mouth was shut (which is not often when I am awake), and when all my defenses were down (ditto).

You know what? The rage dissipated I haven't been angry with my dad since. I understood what God was doing. Can you believe that? What I thought was so wrong and so ungodly was actually being used by God to create the passion and pursuits in my life that I thought my dad had nothing to do with. Carrying all that anger for so many years, rather than trusting God in my own family issues, was such a waste. Silly me.

This greater understanding transformed the way I approach conflict and allowed me not to be controlled by the seemingly devastating events in my past. That same transformation is the right path for you to take on your journey with your child today. While you may think you are in your child's life to help him change, the truth might be that God placed your child (and all her struggles) in your life to change you. That's an interesting thought, is not it?

A young lady asked me not long ago, "What's the worst thing that ever happened in your life?" My answer after a little reflection was this: "There is no worst thing. I now see how God used each of those miserable, dark times in my life; and I would not give up the lessons I learned or the good that came out of each incident, happening, or situation." This perspective changes the way I see everything, and it will change the way you view your child, his or her struggles, and the pain your family is experiencing.

True Stories

Throughout this book I will tell stories about families and different kids who lived with us through the years. We all learn from mistakes others made, and through their stories we find answers to hard questions and hope in some pretty dark times. Before we jump into the next chapter, let me introduce you to five of these kids. Perhaps one of these young people resembles your child and reflects what you are experiencing. (Please note that while the stories and situations are true, the real names and some of the details have been changed to protect each family's privacy.)

Gracie

Gracie's parents were committed to protecting their child from "the world," dedicated to spending as much time with her as possible during her formative years, and devoted to homeschooling her with Christian curriculum. This was an honorable, well-intentioned, thought-out track. A great relationship ensued. Gracie benefited from the good curriculum and developed a good sense of security. She was outstanding at church and an excellent athlete.

As she entered adolescence, Gracie's parents wanted her to become more socially exposed. They allowed her to start public school in the ninth grade. The result was a mess. Because she did not fit in with her peers, she went to extremes to gain their acceptance. Gracie became sexually active within months of going to school and drank because of the dares of her peers. Within six months her language was terrible, her demeanor hateful, and her love for God diminished. Her family's worst fears materialized. Their loving, beautiful daughter turned dark and vulgar.

Michael

Michael's parents knew since he was two years old that something was not quite right. He was always different. Always in trouble. Always an outcast. Always at odds with other kids and teachers. Regardless of the punishment he received or the consequences he experienced, Michael always pushed the edge and stepped over the line.

As Michael entered adolescence, he became enlightened to his awkwardness and began to use drugs and alcohol to self-medicate his relational pain. The drugs led to more and more poor choices that eliminated him from just about every positive activity that could affirm him. He was failing school. His family felt helpless and frustrated as they watched him deteriorate, spiraling into despondency.

Erica

Just one of those normal kids, involved in everything and loved by everyone, Erica was the pride of all—her teachers, her family, her church, and her coaches. She had an engaging personality and witty intellect. Her love for the Lord was encouraging, her love for her family heartening. Her parents were involved in the church and required that she be also, participating in everything and involved every time the church doors were open.

Seemingly overnight, Erica woke up a completely different person. Everything changed, and not just a little. She changed drastically. A few months later, her parents found out she was being sexually molested by their church's youth minister.

Brian

Brian was adopted from another country. About a year after the adoption, when he was four, his parents realized their son was a mess. Nothing seemed to work. He would not or could not bond with his parents. There was always some distance. The doctors called it "reactive attachment disorder." His parents called it disappointment and hurt. Never had something so well-meaning gone so bad. Never a hug, never a response, always wanting to be left alone. When Brian came to us, his connection to life finally began through interacting with a horse named Mariah.

Alan

Alan was a typical attention-deficit kid, always bouncing around to different things. His intellect made him capable of anything. Alan dove headfirst into everything he did, running a hundred miles an hour. When he played baseball, he was the best, but his career was short-lived. When he played the guitar, he wowed people with his talent, but only momentarily. When he decided to become a skinhead, he scared his family, but only temporarily. When he rode and roped on horseback, he was daring and magnificent, but fleeting at best. The low point came when Alan and his dad had it out. In the resulting argument, Dad moved some of Alan's belongings into the front yard.

Alan ran into the house and took a hammer to everything in sight, breaking and destroying his parents' belongings and their home. When Alan's father called the police, Alan ran upstairs and swallowed a bottle of pills. After he was admitted to the adolescent psychiatric ward at a local hospital, his father called me. I met Alan and realized this was a lovable kid who wanted good things but did not know how to get them.

Do any of these stories sound familiar? Perhaps they, like other stories in this book, are being replicated in your home today. Let me assure you if they are, they are not above God's reach or His concern. Nothing is. Your child is still the same child you brought home from the hospital nursery with excitement and joy. Your child is still the same bubbly child who used to make you laugh and make your heart jump for joy. Your child is still the same one you poured your time, heart, money, and life into. He may be going through a difficult time, but he's still that same child, and your investment of time and effort has not been lost. She may seem like a completely different person, but she's not. God has not abandoned you or your child.

Your family can survive and grow through your teen's struggles.

Working through this difficult time with your child is not an easy task. But it will be worth the effort. It may not look the way you planned or feel the way you always hoped it would, but you just might be surprised on the other side of this hardship. That is when you will see how God walked with you and your child through the whole journey, moving you to a better place than you ever dreamed.

CHAPTER TWO

DON'T LOSE HOPE

Each of the young people and their families in the previous chapter experienced a situation that was different from the others. Each was dealing with unique issues and family backgrounds.

But something happened in each that was similar. During the journey with their children, each family identified a problem. Each remained engaged with their children, even when it was excruciatingly painful. Each continued to move toward their children to help and did not allow their children's behavior to control them or detract from their love for their children.

They worked to understand their children and became part of the process of healing rather than fighting against their child. They offered a lifeline of hope to their children, a hope of restored relationship and a hope of getting through the tough times together, regardless of what was happening in the moment.

Working through the struggles with their children led to a deeper relationship with their children and with God. All of them developed deeper understanding of His grace and His plan for their lives. In each situation, the parents maintained a relationship with their child and tackled the hard stuff. Consequently, they validated what they instilled in their child in the earlier years.

In nearly every case, the process ended up better than the parents thought it would. Why? Because the young people I know want their parents—who stood with them when everything was going well—to stand with them when things are not going so well. In other words, teens wonder, *Will you still love me when I don't behave the way you want me to? Good question.*

My wife was sexually abused as a child. It's a terrible story that lasted seven years. With the support of her family, our family, and friends around her, Jan got to the other side of it. Though it was awful and messed Jan up for years, those who loved her stood with her, and she was able to overcome the trauma and become a beautiful woman of God.

Amazingly, the things I love most about Jan are those characteristics, attitudes, and unique personality traits that developed in her because of the abuse. The things I love the most came out of what I hated the most. Paul was not kidding when he wrote that God can make "all things work together for good …" (Romans 8:28 NKJV).

True Hope

I wish I could tell you that every one of the kids I mentioned in the last chapter is doing well now. That would be false hope. I also wish I could tell you that in only a few months, things will turn around and your child will stop messing up. That would also be false hope. I wish I could assure you that your child's struggles are just momentary. Once again, that would be holding out false hope. Then what can I give you? True hope.

Of course, each one of those could happen. But expectations should not be the basis of your hope. Why not? Because true hope is not based on behavior or the timing of our struggles. The true hope I can impart is this: God is involved in your situation. Our hope is in God. Even though your child is going through a tough time, God has not left you, ignored your family, or neglected you.

Let me remind you that Scripture tells us in Proverbs 16:9 that a man's heart plans his way, but God directs his steps. God is with you every step of the way! And remember Jeremiah 29:11: "'For I know the plans I have for you,' declares the Lord, 'plans to prosper you and not to harm you, plans to give you hope and a future.'"

As a parent I would encourage you to grasp this truth:

God's plan for your family is not thwarted because of your child's choices or because your plan is not working.

He is still directing your family's path, and His plans for you are still His plans for you. In fact, He may have chosen you to engage in a painful process that He will use to bring about great things for your child.

A New Perspective

We recently remodeled our home. The three-month project lasted nearly eighteen months, and costs exceeded projections by more than 50 percent. Throughout the project we met workers I now consider friends. They are people I admire and feel blessed to have gotten to know during this long process.

Yes, some of the workers became friends. Others took advantage of us. They lied to us, conned us, made horrendous mistakes, broke promises, and caused much pain and hardship. Jan and I asked questions and expressed our doubts throughout the project: "Why in the world is this happening this way?"; "I thought we did everything right, didn't we?"; "How can people ignore everything we spelled out for them?"; and "Why has something that was supposed to be so easy become so hard?" Sound familiar?

Then Jan and I realized what God was doing. Years ago, we prayed to be involved in the lives of people who were struggling. God was honoring our prayers, bringing these struggling people to us. He did not just bring the ones we wanted. He brought others we never expected. I have no doubt He will continue to bring people into our lives at our expense.

A word to the wise: Be careful what you pray for.

In our remodeling project, what I thought was an inconvenience was really an opportunity. What I thought was wrong was an opening to share what was right. What I thought was unfair really is not that big of a deal now. And the house? It looks better than I thought it would. I learned once again that when you arrive on the other side of any issue, the problem looks smaller in hindsight, and the promises of God remain true. He amazes me, and He amazes me the most when opportunity is born out of confusion and struggle.

Maybe your relationship with your child feels like my home remodeling project. Perhaps what you thought would be a momentary misstep turned into a long-term battle. If so, I want to challenge you to look at your current circumstances from a different perspective. Conflict and struggle bring about changes.

As a matter of fact, conflict is a precursor to change.

As the parent of a teen who is struggling, you have undoubtedly prayed for God to help you become the parent He called you to be. Well, that is just what He is doing now! See this time as a tremendous opportunity to build into your child's life, trusting God to direct your path along the way. Now is your chance to be used, at a time when you are needed the most. Don't back off from the role He gave you, the role you have been practicing for all your life. Develop a mind-set that is consistent with God's—that He has your child's life planned—so you will be able to develop a deeper relationship with your child during this difficult time and shorten the amount of time your child remains in the dark.

Your perspective on what is happening within your family is key. Your correct understanding of your role is necessary. Your willingness to hang in there during this tough time demonstrates perseverance at its best. Your commitment to be a part of God's plan for your child, whether you can see His plan or not, is godly. Loving your child in difficult times shows your true love. Your knowledge that God is involved in your family is the mirror of hope to keep reflecting His love to your child.

If you will keep this perspective, you can have genuine hope that your child can get to the other side and your relationship can be restored.

The Path to Restoration

Even though your heart cries today for your relationship with your child to be restored, restoration takes time and effort. Rarely is it an easy process. In fact, it takes a committed, unwavering perseverance. Scripture tells us in Galatians 6:9, "Let us not become weary in doing good, for at the proper time we will reap a harvest if we do not give up." So don't give up.

And keep a proper frame of mind. When you begin to think about your child and what he or she has been involved in behaviorally, it's usually worse than you think but never quite as bad as you can imagine. Every difficulty can be overcome, and every relationship can be restored. I truly believe that.

Another key to the proper frame of mind is to understand that what is happening right now is not the whole story. The whole story is the role your child is playing in God's story, and the role he is going to play when he gets to the end of himself. God's plan for your child is taking place on His stage, in His timing. Be watchful, prayerful and hope-filled. The fat lady is not singing yet.

Finally, don't panic. You probably feel alone in this whole mess. I can assure you, you are most definitely not. Just because people are silent does not mean other families get by without challenges. Remember, everyone experiences hard times.

I discovered parents usually get pretty scared when a child begins to struggle. Moms have a tendency to get emotional and want to fix things. Dads have a tendency to walk away, as if their inability to fix everything immediately is a sign of their lack of manhood. Parents may feel inadequately prepared to tackle these new challenges. They may have unresolved issues in their own lives. A child could be bringing old skeletons out of the family closet. The struggle is just more than some parents feel they can handle, and they are exhausted.

Inadequacy, new challenges, unresolved issues, old skeletons, exhaustion—that list would scare anyone! This might be the perfect time to place these things in God's hands, trusting He will cause all things to work together for good. If you do, you will already be on the path to restoration.

The only true hope is that God is involved in what is going on with your child. His plan is not determined by what you or your child can or can't see. You and I know God's hand has been involved in the past, and we know it will be in the future, but our difficulty comes in believing He is involved in what is happening today. Just remember what C.S. Lewis once said: "We are not necessarily doubting that God will do the best for us: we are wondering how painful the best will turn out to be."[1]

It's quite amazing to me that through the years more than three thousand teens lived with us at Heartlight. That's almost as many kids as the population of some of this country's largest high schools. I learned thousands of lessons from these teens and families, but first and foremost stands a truth that proves itself over and over again. That truth is this: My job is to offer myself and my skills to help kids get to a place they want to be in life. And to keep them from ending up in a place they never want to go. This is basically the definition of discipline in the teen years.

The value of what I offer cannot be determined by their willingness to accept it. The measurement of my effectiveness is not whether they accept, but the way in which I offer.

What I learned is that the focus of a parent's job is to offer, and to offer in such a way that attracts a teen's interest and conveys a message of hope in her life. It is to communicate, "I am here to help you get through this crazy time called adolescence." I

---

[1] The quote is from one of C.S. Lewis's letters, written to the Reverend Peter Bide on April 29th, 1959. Bide was the Anglican priest who did a 'laying on of hands' healing for Joy Lewis in 1957, and he was also the one who performed the religious wedding of Jack and Joy Lewis (they had earlier had a civil wedding). In 1959 Bide's wife was diagnosed with cancer, and he wrote Jack Lewis to ask him to pray for her. The quote comes from Lewis's response. The letter is in the old (1966) one volume *Letters of C. S. Lewis*, edited by Warnie Lewis.

know this to be true. Your teen wants hope just as much as you do. Maybe more.

Naturally, there are many other things I must do as a parent. First and foremost, I have to make sure I have my teen's best in mind. I should also present my best to my child so she might one day embrace my suggestions, proposals, wisdom, and truth. Let me add something else important here: I don't need kids to embrace my offering. I want them to do so. There is a difference. The need part indicates my need as a parent. The focus is on me. If I want kids to desire and heed the wisdom I offer but my happiness does not depend on it, then I am thinking of their welfare, not my own.

Teens are keen to the motivation of parents.

They know when you are really out for them, and when your parenting style is really for yourself. They see plainly when you act out of your own anger or need something to feed your own sense of worth, reputation, or self-image. If your motivation is to be a "good parent," chances are your child will sniff you out and know you are more motivated to accomplish your program than to develop real relationship. If your motive is to help them get to a better place (and keep them from a place they don't want to go), they can smell that sweet fragrance a hundred miles away and come running as fast as they can.

It's hard to fake hope to one who is hopeless. Hopelessness hurts, but it also sharpens the vision to see genuine caring and real honesty when offered. My prayer for you, my friend, is that you take this time when you feel hopeless to search with your whole heart. I pray you ask God for the answers you so desperately seek, and that your eyes will be filled with light so you may know the hope to which He has called you. He promises to finish what He started. He remains the same yesterday, today, and forever; so those promises remain intact. He will cause all things to work together for good. And Scripture's assurance in Galatians 6:9, "Let us not become weary in doing good, for at the proper time we will reap a harvest if we do not give up" (NIV), has not changed.

Hang in there, my friend. Your story is just like this book. There are many more chapters to come.

CHAPTER THREE

UNDERSTANDING AND WISDOM

As you begin dealing with a struggling teen, you immediately realize the need for understanding and wisdom. Let's consider a few of the basics that will be foundational as you build or rebuild your relationship with your teen.

Face the Right Direction

An old Chinese proverb tells us the journey of a thousand miles begins with a single step. I would add that you might want to make sure you are stepping in the right direction.

Sadly, too many parents today move in the wrong direction with their children. And they are exhausted. If you are already tired and feel abandoned by a child who is struggling, you certainly don't want to get lost as well. As with any journey, a little bit of planning ensures you will get to the right destination. The first priority is to make sure you are pointed in the right direction: loving your child, focusing on him or her, discerning what God may be doing, and avoiding condemnation.

During my years of involvement in Young Life (an organization that reaches out to lost teens), I told gospel stories every week. One of the stories that always caught my attention in a special way was of the woman caught in adultery in John 8. I always wondered what Jesus was writing in the sand when the crowd of religious leaders stood around her, condemning her and planning to stone her to death.

You probably remember that when the Pharisees brought the young girl to Jesus, they told Him they had caught her in adultery and the law required them to stone her. They then asked Him what He would do. His response was to stoop down and write in the sand. Then He stood up and said, "He who is without sin among you, let him be the first to throw a stone at her" (John 8:7). Then Jesus stooped back down and began writing again. He wrote twice. And her accusers dispersed. No one picked up a stone and hurled it. Every one of them walked away. I think I know what Jesus wrote.

We obviously don't know for sure, but I bet He scribbled two simple and intriguing words the first time he wrote in the sand: "What if … " Those two words could hold anyone's interest for just a minute. After He wrote the words, capturing everyone's attention, He stood up, stated His decision, and returned to writing on the ground.

The second time He stooped to write, I think He finished His question: "What if … this was your daughter?" At His spoken word, the rocks hit the ground. And with His sand-scribbled words, the jaws of every father in the crowd dropped. They probably also dropped their pride as they shuffled away, struggling to hold back the tears welling beneath their brows.

People always ask if this is true, if these were really the words Jesus wrote. And they ask if this woman was really a young girl. I don't know, but that's my gut feeling. I have read the story hundreds of times, and I have witnessed a common scenario between fathers and daughters often. Young girls freeze when confronted; older girls run. This girl stood there long enough for Jesus to share His liberating declaration.

Scripture says the older men left the area first, followed by the younger men. Some say the older men left first because they recognized their own sinfulness. I wonder if it was also because many of them were dads. As the younger men followed, they may have asked, "What did He write back there?"; "Why are you so quiet?"; or "Did I just miss something?" You bet they did.

Seeing your child in a traumatic situation like that can get you facing the right direction. It can move your heart toward someone in your family who is struggling. I know from personal experience—a painful personal experience with my son.

Adam

My son Adam made a terrible mistake. He fell in love with a girl. The problem was that Adam was already married. We welcomed his wife into our family when they tied the knot the year before. Their divorce was finalized close to their second anniversary. Now, I loved my daughter-in-law. Adam's decision to divorce closed the door to a lifetime with a daughter-in-law every father would want. The entire experience was painful. It hurt many, including me. It tempted me to judge and condemn my son.

I was shocked this could be happening to me and my wife, angered that my son pulled such a stunt, and infuriated over his timing. Didn't he realize how this would impact our family and hers? Frankly, I was embarrassed at his choices. I performed the wedding and spent quite a bit of time with her family. They loved my son, could say nothing wrong about him, and were excited about this new union. When Adam betrayed their trust, the perfect son-in-law suddenly became a stranger who violated any integrity he possessed.

Having a son offend so many people was a whole new experience for me. Never had I felt such pride turn to shame. I never felt the need to avoid people before. Now I did, hoping they would not ask. I never felt so confused by one of my children's actions. I felt hurt and violated in a way I rarely experienced.

I always told Adam he could never do anything to cause me to love him less. Now he put my words to the test. I was amazed how lost I felt. At the same time, I felt an overwhelming urge to pray for guidance, seek wisdom, and see with the eyes of my heart. I quietly stayed misplaced for a while (about six months), realizing as each day passed that regardless how much control I have over my own life, I have no control over others' lives, including my son. Instead of focusing on what I no longer had, I began asking how God might use me in the midst of this disaster.

My son would continue to be my son. As painful as it was at that time, I needed to continue to be his dad. Our situation taught me in a whole new way that no family is immune from such a struggle. Not mine. Not yours.

I find it intriguing that immediately after the story of the woman caught in adultery, Jesus said this: "I am the Light of the world; he who follows me will not walk in the darkness, but will have the Light of life" (John 8:12). I would have to say if that young woman's dad was in that crowd, Jesus's comment may have been directed right at him. That dad just encountered his child's sin. He was living in the darkness only a sinful child can bring. He needed the Light.

My world is not impregnable, and neither is yours. This kind of situation can happen to you, to those you love, and to those you know, regardless of how much you believe otherwise. This side of Heaven, no family or child is immune to struggle.

Grasping the Truth Is Not Easy

When a child struggles—and you accept that this can happen to your child—the way you look at just about everything changes. Embracing the truth in this time is not an easy thing.

But if you will, your perspective changes. You realize your child or your family never was perfect. Your child's adolescent years tend to bring out some hidden imperfections. Realizing things are not as right as you thought will help you move from judgment to compassion and from harshness to tenderness.

Over the years, I have seen that when parents admit problems exist within their own families, they often change the way they handle situations. They react in a kinder, gentler, and more compassionate way.

Embracing the truth is not easy. It can be downright hard. But when you admit and accept what is happening within your family, you take a major step toward your family's healing. American psychologist and philosopher William James said it this way: "Acceptance of what happened is the first step to overcoming the consequence of any misfortune." Here are some families that came to their realizations in different ways.

John and Virginia

John and Virginia always strived for good things for their two daughters. They lived for their kids and dedicated themselves to being involved in all their daughters' activities. You could always find them at church, giving their kids everything.

Laughter filled the house. Holidays were great. Vacations were wonderful. Pictures throughout the house reflected the depth of the relationships in this family. Everyone in Phoenix knew them as a perfect family.

Then John called me late one night. His first words quivered as they came out of his mouth, "Mark, it's worse than I thought."

Patty, their seventeen-year-old daughter, came home high from smoking pot. In her stupor, she shared with them how she had been doing this for a couple of years, and she stated they could do nothing about it. I listened as John shared what was clearly a double dose of bad news. The first dose was the initial shock that their daughter even knew what pot was and she was smoking it. The second was she had been smoking for quite some time. This loving dad's words to me were filled with hopelessness, and my eyes filled with tears. John's difficult realization came as a shock, and it broke his heart.

Pete and Jennifer

Pete and Jennifer called and asked if they could meet with me. I had met with them off and on during the past year. They kept me informed about their son, Kyle. During this meeting, the conversation began, "Well, we want to let you know what has been happening, catch you up, and get some advice."

Within the past week, Pete and Jennifer discovered their son smoked dope in his room. Then he got into a fight with his mother in the car and called her every name in the book. He threatened to leave home and wanted to drop out of school. For months I had listened to these well-meaning parents describe the ongoing saga with their son, but they never followed any of my advice or directives. When they finally asked what I thought, I decided the time had come to wake them up. We had spent quite a bit of time together, and now was the time to bring some light to a dark subject. I had won the right to be heard. This time, it appeared they were really listening.

I shared that I had seen their son deteriorate during the past ten months. At first, he was struggling through some normal teen issues. Now he was brash enough to smoke dope in his parents' home, showed signs of depression, had wrecked two cars, got arrested three times, lost two jobs and was flunking school. He took his troubles out on his family, yelling and screaming at them. He had turned into a vulgar and hateful young man. I told these parents if they did not wake up and do something quickly, their son would be dead. Probably soon.

As difficult as this was to hear, Pete and Jennifer broke down crying as their eyes were opened by someone who could give them perspective. They did not want to see the truth because it would reveal they failed somewhere. It meant they did not have a perfect family, a perfect child. Where John and Virginia's realization came as a shock, Pete and Jennifer's realization came as enlightenment.

Steve and Tonia

Steve and Tonia adopted a little girl and a younger boy with high hopes for both. But with their adopted son, Adam, things were less than ideal. Adam began to act out, and instead of experiencing consequences for inappropriate behavior, Adam received accolades and applause for anything good. Steve and Tonia did not confront Adam's unacceptable behavior. They believed in "powering him through" his struggles with encouragement to do better. Meanwhile, Adam's occasional visit to the principal's office upgraded to visits by the local police.

Steve and Tonia believed their son was not capable of doing anything bad. This mentality allowed Adam to continue to violate just about every rule and boundary. As Adam's parents believed the fantasy that their son could do no wrong, Adam plummeted in every area of his life—he could do no right. By minimizing the problems, they actually allowed them to grow.

I am not sure what awakened Steve and Tonia. I remember Steve saying, "I can run a company of ten thousand people around the world, but I can't figure out how to help my only son who lives in my own home." Adam paid the price for their blindness, and they eventually had to wake up to their responsibility for what they would not see. Rather than a shock or enlightenment, Steve and Tonia experienced an awakening.

Sam and Marty

Sarah was always a difficult kid. From the day Sam and Marty adopted her they knew something was different. She did not connect with other kids. She was very bright in every way, but she could not stay out of trouble. Throughout grade school and junior high, she was always pushing the limits, manipulating situations and people, refusing to accept responsibility for her actions, and making excuses.

Sam and Marty inherited these issues. They had no control over them, and they were not going to be able to correct or prevent

Sarah's behaviors without professional help. Their love for Sarah was deep, and they soon realized that the "Sarah project" was going to last a long time, so they prepared as best they could. They moved from counselor to psychologist to psychiatrist with all sorts of testing. Rarely have I seen parents willing to do so much with so little return.

Sarah got in trouble at a church youth retreat for taking pills, and that was the straw that broke the camel's back. Sam and Marty felt that if they did not get Sarah to a residential setting that could control her—and hopefully help in the process—she would not live to reach her eighteenth birthday. Their realization of the problem was not a shock, awakening, or enlightenment. It was a validation of what they already knew.

James and Laura

Tammy was the perfect child. Never in a million years would anyone imagine this young girl struggled with some very dark issues. After years of keeping it secret, Tammy tearfully confessed that her uncle was sexually abusing her.

Feeling angry and violated, James and Laura struggled with a confusing set of emotions and beliefs. They loved Tammy, and they burned with anger at the once-trusted family member. They privately beat themselves up over and over, hoping to find solace but really trying to convince themselves they did everything possible to protect their child.

Their realization of their child's problems and struggles came through exposure. Exposure to something new and foreign. They went to sleep in one world, with a joyful thankfulness for their daughter, and awoke the next day to a world of confusion and bewilderment.

Other parents come to the truth through an acceptance of what they already know but find hard to believe, and some parents eventually come to an agreement as Mom and Dad figure out something is wrong and needs to be done to correct what is spinning out of control.

Shock, enlightenment, awakening, validation, exposure, acceptance, and agreement. All different ways of discovering some of the same unpleasant truths. Truths about the damaging behaviors your child is experiencing or engaging in.

From Acceptance to Understanding

Regardless of how parents come to the realization their teen is struggling, the truth is never easy to accept. But as soon as most parents accept their plight, they want to understand what is happening. They desire to find answers and a solution to their predicament.

I have told people this a thousand times: Now that you know the truth, you are in no worse place than you were before you knew it. You just know now. Bad news is never fun to hear, but it gives you the opportunity to do something about it!

Understanding Changes Your Perspective

Perspective is such an important principle. Let me illustrate it for you.

Let's say a man stumbles into a room where I am giving a talk. His speech is slurred as he awkwardly moves towards me. He falls down before me and throws up all over my shoes. With garbled words, he struggles to tell me how sorry he is. He then passes out and falls on my feet.

Most people's first response would be to think he is drunk, and someone ought to keep bums like him out of the room. Most on-lookers would get angry. Others might feel embarrassed. Some might get mad enough to want to drag this drunk out back.

Then I tell you one small detail that might change your perspective and response. The man is experiencing a brain aneurysm. The symptoms of both states are the same. Knowing it is an aneurysm, not booze causing the behaviors, changes everything. That understanding moves you in ways you would not move otherwise.

Because we now understand what is happening, we don't mind that the man threw up. We don't feel embarrassed. The stench and the behavior don't bother us in the slightest. Matter of fact, we are moved to help the poor guy any way we can.

A woman is brought into an emergency room yelling and screaming at everyone, cussing like a sailor, and throwing ob-scenities at everyone present. Does it matter? Are we going to correct her? Do we refuse to help her because she offends us? Not on your life. Maybe she just broke her back in a car accident, and whatever behavior she displays is born of pain, not rational thought.

These situations are similar to teens' struggles. Their behavior is not right, but the behavior is not the issue. It is a symptom of something greater. When you understand that the behavior is a reflection of something deeper, you will change the way you respond and offer yourself to them.

Understanding and wisdom help you see with the eyes of your heart, to look beyond the surface in order to discover that which is hidden and unseen.

One final word on understanding. I realize our first response to the realization that our child is messing up is usually anger. Anger is an emotional reaction to hurt and confusion. It is a response to what is triggered in us by someone else's actions. Once you realize it is not about you, but about your child, you allow your new understanding to capture those negative emotions. When your anger dissipates, you can love and respond with your heart. A new understanding of your child brings a new sense of appreciation.

The Search for Wisdom

Back to my son Adam.

How did I handle my son during his time of struggle? Not well. While it was very easy to imagine what I would do, or to armchair quarterback a scenario with a good ring to it, no one really has any idea how they will respond to a tragedy with their child. Sure, you can say how you would handle it and muster up enough accumulated wisdom to project what it would be like to look straight into the eyes of danger and despair, but when those eyes are your son's, it is like all wisdom flies out the window. Responses are more knee-jerk and spontaneous than well thought-out.

This is what I told my son when he first told me about his affair and his desire to divorce the young lady we loved. Ready? This is what I said: "Adam, when you can call your father-in-law and share with him how you screwed up his daughter's life and what you are going to do to fix it, then I'll talk to you."

That is the reality of what I said to my son in crisis, the young man I told all his life: "There's nothing you can do to make me love you more, and there's nothing you can do to make me love you less." Now my words came back to bite me.

I said those lines hundreds of times. I use them in seminars and conferences. I advise other parents to make sure their kids know that truth. Now I joke about it when I speak sometimes, because the truth of the matter was I did feel I now loved Adam a little less. During many sleepless nights, I sat thinking about the conflict I was experiencing between what I wanted from Adam and how I really felt.

When I told Adam I would talk to him after he did what I knew was the right thing, I thought it would surely motivate him to change his ways, stop his foolishness, and get his life back in line.

It didn't. Truth be told, all I accomplished was to abandon my son when he needed me the most. When he got lost, I told him to go lose himself more. When he became the sheep that wandered, the lost coin that rolled away, I did not go after him to look for him. The son "with whom I was well pleased" when he was doing well became an outcast relegated to an island of shame and disappointment. I pushed him there. I thought drawing the line was great wisdom, but it was pure foolishness. I shamed Adam, only to discover shame pushes people deeper into their shameful behaviors.

I thought I was doing the wise thing. I told friends not to house him in hopes that living in a rotten hotel would help him see his ways and turn things around. I talked with his friends, and we shared how we should pursue Adam and help him get the right perspective. Those friends even met with him and told him he would burn in hell if he got a divorce.

I talked to people, and most of the counsel I received did nothing but affirm my stupid lack of tact and misguided approach to getting my son's attention. Friends, pastors, and many, many others didn't really offer any wisdom. They offered what sounded good. But it was not wisdom, not on your life.

Finally, I shared with a dear friend what Jan and I were going through with our son. I shared what I told Adam. I think I almost expected a high-five for holding my son "accountable." I didn't get one. Paul looked at me and said, "Well, why did you tell him that? At the time he needed you the most, you threw him under the bus. Is that what God would have said to you?"

I thought about the adulterous woman. What did Jesus do? He did not demand, shame, or hurt her. From that moment on, everything changed for me. I saw my son differently. I started to pursue him. The comments I made began the process of healing, rather than creating more alienation and disgrace (interesting word "dis-grace," isn't it?).

So, let me pass on some of the wisdom I learned when my son did everything differently than I expected and wanted.

Chances are, your best efforts got you stuck in the situation you are in. Please don't read that as my saying you are not capable of doing the right thing. You just don't know exactly what the right thing is. If you knew how to fix everything, you would not be reading this book. I would go a step further in telling you that in order to get out of the situation you find yourself in, you are going to have to rely on more than your best efforts, thoughts, plans and strength.

What sounds good and feels right is not always what is best for the new situation you find yourself in. I am reminded of Proverbs 12:15, which says, "The way of a fool is right in his own eyes" (NKJV). My paraphrase? Just because I think it's right, doesn't mean it is. And if it's not, there must be another way found through the wisdom of God and others.

Here is Proverbs 19:20, another verse that applies well to the situation of dealing with a struggling teen: "Listen to counsel and receive instruction, so that you may be wise in your latter days" (NKJV).

Many ask how I have been able to accomplish what I have in the development of Heartlight, the *Parenting Today's Teens* radio program, books, seminars, and more. The answer is easy for me. I surround myself with men and women who are wise, and who give me various perspectives in many varied situations. But here's the clencher: I trust them when I think that they are right (the easy part). And I trust them when I think that they are wrong (much harder). Because I surround myself with wise folks, I don't have to rely on my own foolishness.

Seek counsel from wise people. Seek advice from those who gained their wisdom through observation, reflection, and experience. Wisdom and understanding coupled together usher in a new sense of hope, an assurance that you will get to the end of this current trial. I guarantee when you apply the wisdom of God and others to the traumas you experience with your teen instead of just your own knee-jerk reactions from your own pain and shame, you will sleep far better at night. And your relationships will start on the path to healing, rather than remain mired in hurt.

CHAPTER FOUR

WERE MY PARENTS REALLY THAT BAD?

*H*ow did you learn to be a parent?

You probably learned from your own parents. That transfer can be "like father, like son." Or it could be more like, "What my dad did, I want to do differently."

I believe both perspectives are true for much of today's generation of parents (and grandparents). Most parents don't want to make the same mistakes they believe their parents made, yet they do want to carry on the relational aspect of parenting.

Let me give you a very personal example. I used to think I had to stand against everything my dad stood for. The generation gap between us was as big as the Grand Canyon. Sadly, we did not spend much time together. We had almost no relationship, discussed little, and hardly interacted at all (except when I was in trouble).

My childhood formed my concept of discipline. If I did something against the rules, I received discipline. That discipline was usually physical. It was pretty simple. My understanding was this: Don't do anything bad, and you won't get nailed. If you do something wrong, Dad will find out. When he gets home from the office, you will get a few licks from the belt.

Mom sold us out, and Dad corrected the problem. They probably learned the system from their parents, who were influenced by other military parents.

I learned you never said anything bad to your mom or dad. Cussing, swearing, and dirty jokes never darkened the doors of our home. Beds were always made. Shoes were always shined. You were always on time. A lot was expected of us:

"Yes, Sir."

"No, Sir."

"Yes, Ma'am."

"No, Ma'am."

"Load up; we're going."

"Clean your plate."

"Comb your hair."

"Stand up straight."

"When you shake someone's hand (the civilian act of a salute), do it firmly."

"Speak only when spoken to."

It was Dad's way or no way. Period. No sissy stuff. Treat a girl like a lady. Keep your closets and "stuff" neat. Take care of your business. Defend yourself. Treat your mom nice.

Sound a little like the military? You bet it did. Respect ran high, but it was a little, okay, a lot, short on the relational side. That shortcoming began to form the basis for the kind of parent I would become.

As I got older, I began to understand what made my dad the way he was. I realized he worked hard at the same job for thirty-eight years to provide for his family because that was the way he thought he showed love to his family. My dad demanded (strongly) because that was the way you were to live. You respected your elders because that's the way it was. Period.

As my dark hair lightens, I hear less, and my eyesight diminishes. But I find that wisdom comes easier. I listen more, and I see more with the eyes of my heart. I understand more about my mom and dad, and I realize that things were not as bad as I thought they were while growing up.

I now realize my dad worked so hard because he grew up during the Depression, and he knew what it meant to have nothing. I never experienced anything close to that. Dad left his junior year of high school to fight a war in the South Pacific. I spent my junior year with my girlfriend (who later became my wife), swimming laps and growing hair.

I now understand that my dad's desire was to provide for his family and to protect all of us. He did both. Food was always on the table, a roof was always over our heads, and we never got attacked.

But when the '60s and '70s came along, we younger people wanted a "whole lotta love." We wanted everyone to "shower the people you love with love." Our music expressed our longing for and new pilgrimage to relationships, something our parents struggled with. The concept of all holding hands, growing long hair, and screaming "peace" during an Asian conflict was confusing for dads like mine who expressed love in other ways like hard work.

My point is we need to understand that our concepts about discipline are usually formed in our childhood. We often react against those things we saw as negative, even though at the time we did not see them that way.

How My Parents Changed My Parenting Style

Because of the way I was raised, my focus when I raised my kids was on relationships, not provision and protection. The pendulum of my parenting swung to the other side.

In fact, I believe that in the last forty-plus years, parents have fallen head over heels toward emphasizing relationship in parenting. Think about it. We are the Starbucks generation. We want a place to sit and have a cup of coffee and talk. We want to be where everyone knows our name. We are determined to have relationships with our kids in extraordinary ways, such as the following:

- We embrace new tools of communication like cell phones, text messaging, e-mail, anything to connect with our kids.

- We give our kids things we never got.

- We do things with our kids our parents never did with us.

- We go on more vacations.

- We chauffeur, shuttling our kids everywhere to do what we could not do.

- We coach teams.

- We hug.

- We volunteer in booster clubs and classrooms.

- We teach Sunday school.

- We homeschool.

- We indulge.

- Fathers push strollers, change diapers, and forsake business deals to spend time with their children.

This generation of parents—for the most part—is revolving its family life around its kids with the goal of better relationships. While that may be a significant improvement in some ways from the tough love and relational distance past generations experienced, it also produced some things we did not anticipate.

The Danger of Moving from Parents to Peers

We should applaud most parents today for their desire to build relationships with their kids, but putting kids at the center of our world is creating more and more self-centered kids. In my work with teens, I find they are often immature and unappreciative of what other people do for them. They want more— even when they have everything given to them.

Tim Kimmel made me chuckle when he was on one of our recent radio programs and used the following analogy to describe kids today, "Most middle class kids are born on third base and live under the delusion they hit a triple," Tim said. Needless to say, entitlement and disrespect run rampant as the two greatest negative aspects of relationship-oriented parenting.

Teens I meet are often disrespectful and quick to say inappropriate things to parents, teachers, and coaches. In fact, kids often say things that would have gotten me knocked halfway into next week when I was a teen. They seldom show appreciation, demand often, want more, and feel little satisfaction. They can't seem to have enough or keep busy enough.

Amazingly, they are angry. They lack a strong work ethic, want instant gratification, and have little motivation to do or become anything much. In some ways, they are helpless. As they move closer and closer to becoming adults, they begin to understand they will need to make it on their own. And they realize they have absolutely no idea how, because they never had to do anything. It was all done for them. Now they feel angry and hopeless.

I don't need to go further. You get the picture. And though I know plenty of exceptions to everything I am writing, we need to understand that as parents we have created an environment we did not anticipate. For the most part, we now have the kind of kids for which we did not prepare. We now feel what our parents felt. Our kids are thumbing their noses at us, just as we thumbed our noses at our parents.

Somewhere along the line we moved from being parents to being peers. That's a very dangerous move, regardless of how well-intentioned it is.

Think about it for a moment. Barking out orders is pretty easy when we are the boss. Giving direction is simple when we are the director. Correcting someone is relatively painless when we are in a position of respect. Correcting a peer is harder.

When we are peers to our kids (more of a peer-ent than a parent), we stand on equal ground with them. This has the potential to create stronger relationships with our children, but it undermines our position of authority. I am not saying we should be authoritarians, but we do need to strive for a position in our children's lives where we offer something more than their peers offer. When I encourage parents to have a relationship with their teens, I am not saying they should become friends. Most teens have those. What they need is a parent who is relational, not authoritarian, in approach.

So the big question is this: How do we regain the position of respect we abdicated while maintaining the relationships we worked so hard to develop with our kids? Can we do both? Can we exercise authority and at the same time build a strong relationship with our kids? Yes! In fact, as we pursue this balance in parenting, I believe we learn to love our kids in a deeper way and develop an even stronger relationship with them.

"Mark," I hear you saying, "How do I do that?"

You start by telling them, "As your parent, I will stand beside you and walk with you. But make no mistake; I will stand in front of you when I need to."

As I mentioned in an earlier chapter, discipline entails helping your child get to where he wants to be and at the same time keeping him from a place he doesn't want to be. Take a moment to think about that because it is simple, yet profound.

To pull this kind of parenting off, you have to be strong when you need to be strong and tender when you need to be tender. It's not either/or; it's both/and. A healthy parent knows when to do one or the other and when not to do either.

This kind of balance not only makes you a better parent, it also reflects the very character of God. In the book of Isaiah we are told He is like a mighty warrior (Isaiah 42:13). Yet in that same book we read, "As a mother comforts her child, so will I comfort you" (Isaiah 66:13 NIV). Tough and tender. Strong and sweet.

God embraces both characteristics, feminine and masculine. He is a God of power and a God with a great sense of tenderness. If one of our purposes as parents is to give our kids a taste of the character of God, then we must be tough when we need to be and tender when it is appropriate.

If you have never been firm with your children, being tough with them will probably be difficult. But your kids desperately need this kind of parenting. You will never be successful if you are unable to set boundaries and be strong with your children.

On the other hand, if you have never been tender with your child, you need to start that today. Your kids will have a difficult time accepting your new desire for warmth and gentleness, but it's never too late to start.

Balance and Focus in Discipline

Many parents do not discipline their children because they are afraid they will become like that military father they swore they would never be. Others do not discipline because they are afraid of losing the good relationship with their child they worked years to attain. Then there are parents who flat-out don't know what to do because they think everything has gone so well. They cannot imagine their child could do wrong. As a result, they could be blindsided when their child requires some behavioral changes, consequences, or boundaries.

Most parents are simply unprepared for the teen years. They do not easily move from the lecture method to the discussion method. They are reluctant to give their kids more freedom. They are surprised when they catch a glimpse of adolescent rebellion on occasion. They feel abandoned when their kids begin to move away from them socially.

At the core, the teenage years are a time of change. You need to be prepared for that change. You need to understand the new world your teen moves into. If you do, you will be ready, rather than caught with your guard down.

Making that transition can be a real challenge. Raising our kids by doing everything for them is easy. We enjoy knowing that, for the most part, they think we can do no wrong. But as kids get older, things change, don't they? They go off to sixth or seventh grade and find they are not as cool as they thought they were.

As they move from concrete thinking to abstract thinking, they begin to view their parents differently as well. They begin to realize Mom and Dad are not cool at all. When that happens, things can get confusing for the parent. For example, I am always amazed at how teens can turn an issue about them into an issue about you, pointing out your shortcomings as a parent.

Let's make sure we are clear on this: Discipline's focus is about the child, not the parent. Of course, parents need to deal with some of their own issues, and how you deal with your issues will determine how effective you are in your discipline techniques. But your issues do not give license to your children, at any age, to ignore or neglect the type of discipline that will help them grow.

Teen discipline should target dishonesty, disobedience, and disrespect. Your child should learn these negative traits bring painful consequences. But the positive alternatives bring desirable results:

- Honesty will help them in their relationships in the future.
- Obedience will help them gain direction and insight into life.

- Respect is the bedrock of all friendships and interpersonal relationships.

Your correction of your children over these qualities is vital. Your correction helps them choose and develop the types of relationships they really want, and keeps them from destroying or impeding relationships with their foolishness.

I will add one more note: I always said moms instill a sense of value in a child, and dads validate that sense of value. But I am amazed at how many times I see Mom doing all the discipline these days, with Dad participating very little. Kids pick up one message from these dads: "I don't care about you." Without participation in the discipline of a child, a dad will force a child to find validation somewhere else.

The Importance of Discipline

I don't know any parents who want their children to grow into weak, immature adults. Discipline is not just punishment and the inflicting of pain.

True discipline is about building the character qualities of honesty, obedience, and respect.

I encourage you to embrace your wonderful leadership role in your child's life.

If you are currently struggling with the discipline of your child, I urge you to hang in there. You will eventually get on the other side of this thing called adolescence. A brighter day is ahead.

You can have a deeper relationship with your child than you had with your parents. Just keep putting one foot in front of the other, and do not give up.

John Wayne once said, "Courage is being scared to death but saddling up anyway." It's getting back up in the saddle when you get thrown for a loop. These are true words, especially understood by those of us who have broken or trained horses. The training process begins easy, but it can get pretty ugly.

I have a set practice for breaking and training horses, but I adapt it to each one. The course of action I take brings different reactions from each horse. When one method does not work, I don't think of myself as a failure. I simply start using another technique.

Breaking and training a horse is hard work, but it is worth the effort. I know I will eventually have a great relationship with a horse as it carries me and walks alongside me through many different fields. But to get there, I might get bitten, kicked, knocked down, snorted on, thrown off, pulled back, head butted, beaten up, broken, worn out, pooped on, slammed against fences, walked on, stomped on, and run away from during the process of training. I will end up being dog-tired, my clothes ripped and blisters torn.

The horse will get angry, hostile, obstinate, belligerent, unwilling, unteachable, stubborn, immovable, and inflexible. He may be determined to remain a wild, selfish, self-gratifying, hay-eating, headstrong, and noncompliant equine. I learned through my years of breaking horses that the horse will think the problem is me and my interference in its life.

However, eventually the horse learns it is not about me. It's about him. Over time, he gentles. Knowing this, I keep the process going. Why? Because I really do love the horse even though the process is painful. I know where we are headed.

I sometimes wonder if the reason we see so much anger in young people is that we are not patiently preparing them for the world into which they are walking. Anger is an emotional response to not getting what you want. Young people tell me all the time they are angry, but they do not know why. However, as I spend time with them and help them process what they feel and think, I sense they just are not ready to hit the world running, and their unpreparedness angers them.

Could this be one of the reasons young people headed off to college these days are so dependent on their parents? I would be mad, too, if someone expected me to fulfill an expectation without preparing me for the task.

We must prepare our children for the world in which they will live. As my good friend Tim Kimmel says, "You can raise your teens to live in a zoo, or you can prepare them to survive in the jungle." As we raise our children, our emphasis must switch from protecting to preparing, from lecture to discussion, and from doing things for them to allowing them to do things for themselves.

Teens today are immature because we create a teen world that lacks accountability and is short on responsibility. Parents must move young people from dependency on Mom and Dad to independence. It is part of training. It is part of discipline. It allows for and motivates the maturing of relationships. This shift helps young people "leave and cleave" when the time comes.

Parenting Styles That No Longer Work

No, your parents probably were not that bad. And as products of our environment where the fruit doesn't fall that far from the tree, I am sure we have all picked up some habits from our parents that may have been effective when we were raised, but are no longer applicable to a generation of kids surviving in a culture far different from the environment in which we grew up.

If you really want a relationship (remember, not just a friendship) with your teen, then you must strive to position yourself in a role where that can happen. The first thing on the list is to accentuate the good things happening in your family, and eliminate those things getting in the way of relationships.

The purpose of talking about discipline in the context of what we learned from our parents is to see the delicate balance between authority and relationship as you develop your parenting style. My hope is you are striving to take the best aspects of your parents' style and incorporate them into your parenting style, while forging new and better ways to communicate and relate to your kids. Be intentional about pushing your kids toward maturity by giving them responsibilities and requirements, and by being unafraid to discipline when it is necessary.

Many times, today's parents are utilizing styles and techniques that might have worked years ago, but are no longer effective and applicable for today's teens and their environment. I call it our "parenting baggage." If you are doing things that "provoke your children to wrath" (See Ephesians 6:4 KJV.) or cause them to rebel, changing your approach can alter your teens' response. This is important because the first place to look when trying to figure out why your teen is acting out is at yourself! Yep, you gotta look at the log in your own eye before you look at the speck in your teen's eye. This is where you pray that prayer, *Lord search me, know my heart, and see if there is any hurtful way in me.* (See Psalm 139:23-24.)

You may ask, "Hurtful in what way?" Hurtful to such an extent that your child shuts you out before you have an opportunity to offer her an involved relationship and your shared wisdom.

Kids are looking for wisdom, not more information.

My hope for you is that you will move everything out that is standing between you and a relationship with your child. My prayer is that you will gradually (notice I did not say overnight) move to a place where hurtful ways do not affect your ability to engage and offer the wisdom your child needs.

Parenting Styles that Get in the Way of Relationship

I swore as I got older I would never speak the words "back in the day." But as I age and see the vast differences in generations, I will write about it just this one time.

Back in the day, my dad wanted the grass at our home to be perfect. We never talked about problems, never shared struggles. Our hair had to be combed right, our shoes polished, and our beds made. My mom always looked perfect, and we had to make my parents look faultless and flawless.

Back in the day, my dad was the strong authoritarian you never crossed. His word was final, he was always right, and he never made a mistake or admitted a wrongdoing. We answered directives and questions with "Yes, sir" and "No, Sir" for fear of strict and severe punishment blistering our hind ends if we did not. It was his way. Period. End of story.

Back in the day, what my dad said was truth and there was to be no contradiction of his biased (and sometimes stupid) observations about others, situations, or happenings. The thought of contradicting was pure foolishness. Countering his viewpoints was never allowed.

Our family worked together like a well-oiled unit as long as all appeared perfect, Dad got to be in charge, and we did not question his judgmental comments about life.

That was back in the day. That kind of parenting style is no longer effective.

I never hear moms state they want their daughters to be perfect and have it all together. I have never heard a dad really state he wants to rule his home with an iron fist and be the authoritarian. I have never heard a set of parents state they desire to be judgmental parents. Yet I hear hundreds of young ladies divulge to me their mother demands perfection in everything they do. I hear hundreds of young men share with me how they cannot wait to get away from home because their dad is too demanding and rules with an iron fist. I hear thousands of teens tell me their parents are the most judgmental people they know.

Some of the parental baggage parents carry today is nothing but the antiquated ways of their own parents, even if they mean to parent in the exact opposite manner.

Does any of this sound all too familiar?

CHAPTER FIVE

THE PROBLEM OF PERFORMANCE-BASED RELATIONSHIPS

$\mathscr{T}$he next step on our journey in parenting teens is to deal with the issue of performance-based relationships. Parents must address this significant issue directly because most teens believe people will only love them up to a certain point. Beyond that point, the love is gone. As a result, they strive to do well and never do wrong. Or they lose hope, give up, and rebel.

Their drive is rooted in fear that if they make a mistake or do badly, they will lose those they love. Unfortunately, their perception may contain some truth. This fear is usually fostered in children's younger years and is an extremely difficult way of thinking to break. It develops from the pattern that when they do something bad, they get in trouble, and when they do something good, they get rewarded. The problem in Christian circles of young people can be even worse. As a Christian kid, when you do something bad, you may get eliminated. Leigh was no exception.

Leigh

Leigh grew up with two loving parents who chose her to be in their family when they adopted her as a baby. I met her when she was fourteen, spinning out of control and letting everyone know she was unhappy. Her newfound role in life was to make those around her as miserable as possible.

Leigh set fire to other kids' lockers at school, cussed out teachers, screamed at her parents, flunked every class she was taking, and acted like she was an uppity city girl who did not care about anything or anyone. Her youth minister asked her to leave the youth group.

Her demise came suddenly. Just a year earlier, she was the number-one kid in the youth group. She loved school and always went to summer camp. Then her behavior changed and her youth minister's rejection sent her over the edge. I think it brought out feelings about being adopted she carried for years and did not recognize. Now they were boiling to the surface. Leigh experienced feelings of rejection and abandonment. The better she performed in school and the better she acted in her relationships, the more confused she became about why her birth mother would give her up for adoption.

Her parents were devastated and exhausted. They tried everything to make things work at home and came to the conclusion that unless they got help outside the home, their spunky little ninth grader was not going to make it past her eleventh-grade year. I concurred.

I immediately liked Leigh. I remember the first time I met her parents. Successful. Well-meaning. Sincere. And broken. I liked them too. I hurt for this family. I felt as if I were at my first funeral as her dad shared their story and all they did to help her. My eyes welled up with tears, and I felt as if my heart would break. I kept thinking this could happen to my family. I was torn. I was distraught. I fell in love with the parents as much as I did the young lady who came to live with us at Heartlight.

Leigh had a spunkiness about her. She was verbally interactive. She was a cute little girl who traveled and knew the ropes. She knew how to get her way. I always thought if we could get her a sales job somewhere, she could make us all millions. When she was not cussing me out, she could be a pretty sweet girl.

I spent a year counseling with Leigh. We filled hours and hours of coffee drinking with laughter and tears as we talked about her adoption issues and her fear of not being able to live up to her parents' expectations. I tried to help her sort through her jumbled mess of emotions.

She completed our program and went home to a changed family. Two years later, the ugly serpent's head reappeared, and she wound up leaving home. We were all devastated to see her leave. Months later, her mother called and asked if I would come to Kansas City to help find Leigh and talk with her.

I found a phone number, called her, and took her out to dinner. She ate two full entrees, and I knew her lifestyle was tearing her apart. She was prostituting herself for drugs. She lost her spunkiness and the gleam in her eye. She did not laugh once. Neither did I. Seeing what Leigh had chosen after I had spent so much time with her tore me apart. I could hardly imagine what her parents were going through.

Before I left, we stopped by a McDonalds and I purchased a hundred dollars' worth of gift certificates, not wanting to give her cash but wanting to put food in her belly. Leigh called me months later and asked if I could come see her. She was pregnant and did not know whether to keep the baby. She said she finally wanted to make some changes. I flew to Kansas City the next morning and sat with this young lady who had not only been around the block a few times; but also had lived on its streets, eaten from its cans, and stood on its corners.

Leigh's story was twenty years in the making. She finally turned a corner when she realized her value was not determined by what she did, does, or will or will not do. Leigh finally saw that she was valued during her bad years, not just her good years.

Perception Is Truth to the One Who Perceives It

In performance-based relationships, people are valuable because of their actions, accomplishments, and achievements.

They are accepted because they meet others' expectations. Take a moment and read those statements again because understanding this is critically important.

Performance-based relationships are conditional and convey or withhold love according to one's performance. These types of relationships hold the bar of expectation too high for most to attain and then maintain. When teens fail to meet others' expectations, they experience an overwhelming sense of disappointment, discouragement, despair, and despondency.

Most teens I meet believe they have performance-based relationships with their parents. They believe their parents' love is conditional, based on how they behave.

You may not think this is true with your child, but perception is truth to the one who perceives it. In all my years of working with struggling teens, every young person I have met believes their value is based on their performance. We parents would do well to show our kids that our love is not conditional and assure them we do not want performance-based relationships.

Remember, what your child *thinks* is reality for him or her.

What Do You Communicate to Your Child?

What do you and your teen talk about? My guess is you discuss academics, work, behaviors, rules, privileges, sports involvement, picking the right friends, choosing the right clothes, cleaning up a room, performing chores, and obeying the rules of the house.

Now take a moment and think about what else you talk about. Is it a pretty short list? If so, do you get my point? Most of what we talk about is performance-oriented. This imbalance can create the impression your relationship with your kids is based on how they perform.

Mom and Dad, the separation of performance and relationship is critical. You want your son or daughter to perform well, but performance should have nothing to do with your relationship. Teens need to hear this repeatedly. If they do not understand this, their failures will eventually catch up with them and move them to frustration and futility. We parents must convey our love in ways not based on performance.

We need to help our kids understand our love for them is totally unconditional, just as God loves us unconditionally.

Leigh thought her parents' love for her was based on her performance. Their successful lifestyle conveyed an unspoken demand for Leigh to achieve for their love. Her confusion was not her parents' fault. But parents do need to understand the way their lifestyle, parenting style, and personalities affect their children.

Leigh was already trying to perform. She believed her birth mother rejected her. ("She gave me up, and she didn't even know me," she once said.) Now she was trying to prove her worth.

Every child wants to do well for his or her parents. We have all heard statements like: "This one's for you, Mom," "Make your parents proud," "Don't embarrass your mom," "Win one for dear, ol' Dad," and "Do your best, Son."

Every mom and dad must release their children from living under the fear that love will be taken away if children don't perform.

I am amazed at the negative comments some parents make to their kids. Those words stay with kids. I know because of what teens share with me. Negative words, and sometimes just the absence of positive and affirming ones, can turn out the lights in a child's life. Imagine how kids feel when the most important people in their lives say things like these:

"I am ashamed of you."

"You make me sick."

"Get out of my sight."

"I can't believe you."

"Go to your room and away from me."

"You are out of this youth group."

"How could you do this to me?"

"We never should have adopted you."

Comments like these set kids up for performance-based relationships and make them question their self-worth. They also drive kids to look elsewhere for their validation. Words can plunge a child into darkness. The myth that, "Sticks and stones can break my bones, but words can never hurt me" is a bold-faced lie. I once heard someone say that the root of all mental illness is the fear that love is conditional. That might not be too far from the truth.

Expectations and Performance-Based Relationships

Do parents want good things for their kids? Absolutely. I am not implying you should abandon your high expectations for your children or that you should not encourage them to be the best they can be. Just be careful not to communicate that your love is conditional. Assure them you will always be there for them. I want my children (and now my grandchildren) to know they can do nothing to make me love them less, and they can do nothing to make me love them more. I just love them.

Parents must be careful how they communicate their expectations because every child will fail sometimes. When your children do not perform well, they think your relationship will suffer unless you convince them otherwise.

This is the critical juncture—and often the melting point—of a parent-child relationship. This is often when parents ask themselves how something so well-intentioned (their desire for their child to succeed) could work against them. And kids begin to think they can never live up to their parents' expectations—or God's—so they give up.

Let me give you just one example. Some popular programs motivate kids to save themselves sexually until marriage. These programs are very well-intended. I am sure many kids commit themselves to abstinence and save themselves sexually for the one they someday marry. This is a well-founded expectation, based on biblical truth, agreed to by the teen, and rooted in nothing but a fine attempt to help teens live the way God desires for them to live.

But what happens to those promise makers who become promise breakers? What happens when you no longer fit in the club? What do kids think and feel when they make mistakes that eliminate them from something they have been striving for? Or when they have to lie or fake it to stay in the group and hide their shame?

Of course, kids must experience the consequences of their choices. But sometimes we make those consequences worse than they need to be. We do well when we set high standards for kids to challenge them in activities that will help them be the best they can be. But we do not do well when we set standards that exclude them if they make poor choices. Spelling bees, softball, soccer, and video games are one thing. But when kids break a covenant they made with God, should they be thrown out of the club?

Why am I so concerned? One report stated that 61 percent of those who make a pledge in one of these abstinence programs break their promise. Of those who keep break their promise not to have sexual intercourse, 55 percent engage in oral sex.

My point is not to trash any of these programs. If they save just one person from sexual promiscuity, then they are worth every penny of expenditure. But kids need a Plan B that does not eliminate them when they make poor choices. As I read Scripture, I find nothing that eliminates us from God's family once we come to know Him as Savior. Let us reflect on that when we set our standards.

I conducted a "Tough Guys & Drama Queens" parenting seminar in Nashville and was amazed to hear the pastor of a 2,800-member church tell me the church currently did not have a youth pastor—nor many kids in their youth group.

When I walked into the room where we were holding the seminar, I noticed a set of standards displayed on the wall. The standards were certainly biblical—great expectations put there with the greatest of intentions. Each member of the youth group was to make these commitments:

I will witness to everyone I meet.

I will represent Christ in all I do.

I will not sin and will strive to show Christ's love to everyone.

I will devote my life to serving Him.

I will live my life as an example of the One who died for me.

I will never be selfish and will strive to think of others first.

I will live my life as a sacrifice to Him who loves me and died for me.

I thought, *Man, these are some great expectations and standards.* I also thought, *No wonder kids don't want to be a part of this group!* No one could say anything bad about each of these biblical standards. But what human being could follow every one of them? I can't.

Dan Allender states this in his book *How Children Raise Parents*:

> "We fail when certain standards of behavior, rather than grace and forgiveness, are assumed to be the core of Christianity ... The result of a standards-oriented religion is the rise, if not the dominance, of a self-righteousness for those who appear to be doing what is expected. For those who aren't as adept at deceiving others, the outcome of a standards-driven Christianity will be shame."[1]

It is not that God's standards have become too high for kids. It is just that we eliminate our kids along the way when we do not provide for their continued engagement should they fail. Churches, pastors, youth pastors, and parents must be careful about setting up things that eliminate rather than include people who fall, like your teens – and you.

Grace is undeserved—it is available to those who make poor choices. Forgiveness makes a way for us to include those who fall. If these two points were added to that wall of expectations, that church might have a larger youth group. And the American church at-large might not be losing millions of teens from our youth groups by the time they reach the twelfth grade.

Changing a Performance-Based Relationship

People often ask me how we work with kids, why we are so successful in our approach, and why kids respond to us the way they do. The answer is simple. We love kids when they are at their worst.

Every teen I ever met wants to know he or she will continue to be loved when everything is a mess. You and I know loving is easy when all is going well. It's quite a different matter when everything is spinning out of control.

The first thing to do in the middle of the mess is to move toward your kids, especially if they are struggling and in a tough spot. Let them know you love them regardless. If you do not love them, learn to. Tell them at least every week that you love them not because of what they do but because of who they are.

Second, know that good relationships do not work well with only lists, standards, and expectations. They work well with a love that says, "I love you, period." You may still get disappointed when you face disrespect, dishonesty, or disobedience. You may get frustrated when your child violates promises, acts inappropriately, or flunks a class. You may get mad when your child breaks something, makes mistakes, or deceives and lies to you. But you can still love her. Loving her does not take away consequences. It just means you can separate her actions from the way you love and value her.

Leigh learned through the years that people could love her when she was a mess. My years with Young Life taught me to proclaim the gospel of Jesus Christ across a bridge of friendship and not to stop if kids don't respond. St. Francis of Assisi said, "At all times share the gospel, and when necessary, use words." My love for Leigh has nothing to do with what she has done, what she is doing today, or what she will do. I am just thankful she knows she is loved.

I pray the same is true for your child.

If you want to know if your son or daughter thinks what they do is more important than who they are to you, ask them. Ask them with the intent to know their heart, not to share your opinion. Be prepared for their answer to sting, and do not criticize their thoughts and conversation. Thank them for being open with you, and take their words to heart. Ask them what you could do to make them feel your love unconditionally (besides buy them the latest-and-greatest whatever. This is not about stuff and things. This is about relationship.) Let them know you hear them and will try to do things differently.

Do this right now. Why not text your teen and ask them some questions? You know teens will say things in a text they won't say face-to-face. Go ahead. Ask.

Here are some questions that can help get the discussion going:

- Do you think I am more concerned about the condition of your room than I am the condition of your heart?

- If you could change one thing about our relationship, what would it be?

- Do you know that I love you, really?

- What would you say about spending some time together to talk (not yell) about the stuff that makes us so different?

- Where do you think I miss your heart the most?

- What word would you use to describe our relationship?

- If there is one thing you could change about me, what would it be? Do you think I can ever change?

- Do you think the beginning of mental illness is the fear that love is conditional?

- What are the things you think we differ on the most?

- Where do you see our relationship on the day you get married?

Bring those to the dinner table, or go out and have a cup of coffee and ask your teen to explain her answer. Follow these simple rules. Mom, do not correct her, tell him he is wrong, or share a better way of answering. Dad, do not try to fix anything that might be broken. Convey a message to your child that you still love him, regardless of whether he is fixed, broken, all put together, or a complete mess.

Just opening the door to discussion might convey a message to your teens you are more concerned about listening to their heart than you are sharing what is on your mind. *Just listen.* Then think about how you would like to respond over the next week. You can share some of those thoughts with your child when you get together again. Start the conversation by saying, "Hey, I have been thinking about what you said last week. Here are some of my thoughts. What do you think?"

Teens do not struggle because they like it. I never met one teen who said, "I really like to be a mess," or "I kind of enjoy being screwed up." Never. Teens are messed up for a reason. Just make sure their mess is not because they think their relationship with you is performance-based.

One more time, your teens would rather be loved for who they are, warts and all, than for what they do. Wouldn't you?

CHAPTER SIX

WHY DOES MY CHILD ACT THIS WAY?

*P*arents who bring their out-of-control kids to Heartlight consistently ask, "Why does my child act this way?" They are distraught, exhausted, desperate for help, and trying to get a handle on their children's behavior. They want to stop the downward spiral of inappropriate habits and actions. That first question opens the door to even more questions:

"Why has my child chosen this type of behavior?"

"What is my child trying to accomplish?"

"When did this inappropriate behavior begin?"

"What is my child trying to say?"

"What caused my child to move in this direction?"

"What does my child really want?"

"What message am I supposed to hear?"

"What have I missed?"

"Why am I having a hard time finding answers?"

"Why does he act the way he does?"

"When will this inappropriate behavior end?"

Sound familiar? I am sure it does if your child is displaying mystifyingly new and inappropriate behaviors. Asking questions like these and seeking honest answers is a critical process. It will move you to make some changes in the way you run your home, the way you parent your child, or the way you offer alternatives and opportunities to your teen. Ashley and her parents provide us a great example.

Ashley

When I first met Ashley, she was a ninth grader from upstate New York. As her parents were checking her into Heartlight, I asked if she wanted to take a walk around the property, see the houses and the horses, meet some of the other young people, and get a feel for the place where she was going to spend her next nine months. I was really just looking for an opportunity for her to begin telling me what was going on with her and her family.

As we walked, talked, and had our "meet-and-greet" with other residents, they asked her, "What are you here for?" You would think she had just been convicted and was coming to Heartlight to serve her sentence!

Her answer was quick and compact. Without missing a beat, she said, "I have been drinking and sleeping around. I have been depressed for a couple of years. I started cutting myself, and I can't stand my parents." The answer rolled off her tongue as if rehearsed and practiced.

I am always amazed at how honest young people are about their own behavior. They are completely willing to share with their peers how screwed up they are (even with complete strangers). Remarkably, kids immediately bond in their dysfunction and pain. Birds of a feather do flock together.

Could your child be hanging out with kids who are rotten influences because they can identify with each other's hurts? Could your child be in as much pain as those other kids? I think so.

Perhaps these kids in all their messes are closer to community and connection than most adults. Adults often hide or ignore their behavior and motives rather than express how they really feel. I sometimes wonder how people would respond if I was brutally honest when they ask me, "How you doing, Mark?" I think I would shock most people. Many would be uncomfortable with that much honesty. Deception is easier to handle than reality.

Despite some momentary awkwardness, people tend to communicate more deeply and bond when they share a common hurt. Most churches and youth groups enjoy greater unity when honesty and truthfulness are laid on the table.

Because of Ashley's bluntness and honesty, she immediately connected with her inquisitors and took her first step toward deepening relationships with some future lifelong friends. Her frankness was an open invitation for me to ask some questions. As we sat up at a horse barn surrounded by saddles, lead ropes, and bridles, she began to "pony up" some answers.

The tears that filled her eyes were some of the biggest I had ever seen as she tried to put answers to her feelings and purpose to her thoughts. She continued to open up, so I continued to ask questions.

She shared that her father had been an alcoholic. She wept as she told me her family witnessed her dad's suicide. She painfully revealed that having a new stepdad was a constant reminder of all the things she lost because of her biological dad's death.

She went on to disclose that no one really knew her and she did not know why she was doing what she was doing—except to ease the pain of life. She said she felt confused, alone, lost, worn out, exhausted, and hopeless. I was not surprised. She used the same adjectives her mom and stepdad used to describe the past two years of their lives.

I am still moved by young people's pain, even after forty years of hearing their stories. You would think after hearing thousands of tragic stories, I would not be fazed anymore. But even as I write Ashley's story, I tear up thinking about the pain she went through. Life turned on a dime for her; it changed so drastically in an instant. My heart breaks when I see the sins of a family passed on to the children. I ache when I see well-meaning people ignore the needs of the young people around them, not because they don't want to help but because of their own pain, their own baggage. And because they do not know what teens' real needs are.

All I could say to Ashley as she shared her story was something like this: "Sweetheart, I don't blame you for what you have been doing. I can't imagine what you have been through. If I were you, I might be drinking a little more. But your parents and I can't allow you to continue the path you are on because it will take you somewhere you don't want to be. It might even kill you."

She was quick to remind me she did not want to be at Heartlight either. I let out a laugh and told her I understood. I also shared with her I was glad she did not want to leave home and that she longed to return as soon as possible. I assured her my job was to get her where she wanted to be.

Her behavior obviously was not the issue. Deeper issues were swirling around in Ashley's heart and head. We cannot allow ourselves to be distracted by what is happening to our teen on the surface (the behavior); we need to look deeper into teens' lives and understand the motivation behind the behavior. Behavior is never the issue. It always points to something bigger.

All Behavior Is Goal-Oriented

If behavior is never the issue, then what is? Our task is to understand what prompts the behavior.

Before I go any further, I want to instruct you not to ignore your child's inappropriate behavior. You cannot justify its existence or allow destructive behavior to continue. However, if you focus solely on the inappropriate behavior and do not try to figure out the reasons why they behavior is occurring, you teen will not experience true healing. Your family will not experience true healing. You may stop the destructive behavior, but behavior modification alone will never reach the heart. The real issues lie in the heart hurts.

Unless kids' hearts are changed, most of them will return to their old behavior when they go back to their old environment. .

How do you touch the heart of a troubled teen? You start by understanding that behavior is always driven by a goal. This means you have to ask what the goal is. What do kids hope to accomplish through their actions?

- They want something.
- They want someone to hear their message.
- They want someone to take notice.
- They want to show their maturity and independence.
- They want to cover up the pain of an incident or trauma.
- They want to find acceptance.
- They want to know that they are more than the rejection they feel.
- They want relief.

Make no mistake—kids' behavior is driven by a goal. Unfortunately, struggling teens may not even know what that goal is, They may have no clue why they do what they do when they are doing it. Usually, the more bizarre the behavior, the more desperate the child is to find a remedy. A child's behavior then becomes an indicator of the depth of the issue she is seeking to resolve and of the lengths she is willing to go to in order to reach her goal.

Ashley's bizarre behavior was shouting to all that her struggle was much more than poor behavior. Ashley was attempting to resolve her issues related to her father's suicide, numb the pain of all she felt, and get some relief from the visual images stuck in her head. Those were her goals. She chose the behaviors available to her.

The progression is pretty easy to understand but most difficult to decipher.

- The behavior reflects the goals.
- The goals represent a logical but perhaps subconscious plan to meet a need.
- The need reflects the true intent of the behavior and actions.

When I say "needs," I mean those real or perceived conditions, possessions, environments, relationships, or actions that are essential or desired to fill an area where something is lacking or unattainable.

One of the reasons this seemingly simple system is actually quite complex is that an out-of-control teen's needs are usually hard to sort out. Even when you are able to accurately identify those needs, prioritizing them is always a challenge.

Neither Ashley nor her parents knew what her actual needs were. Her behavior was easy to understand. Who wouldn't be doing crazy things when people did crazy things to them? But understanding a child's situation does not mean you have to agree with the behavior. Nor does it give a child license to continue in the inappropriate behavior.

I commonly tell kids, "I understand where you're coming from." At times, they interpret that to mean I believe they are justified in what they are doing. I am quick to remind them I understand, but quicker to remind them the behavior must stop. Ashley hated her mom and stepdad because they were keeping her from inappropriately coping with her issues. Sure, they were issues she did not choose, but she certainly had a choice in how to handle them.

We can easily understand why Ashley chose the behaviors she did. They were available to her. Drinking, cutting, and sleeping around became her coping mechanisms. If her parents or those of us at Heartlight were going to get to the heart of Ashley's issues, we were going to have to look beyond the inappropriate coping mechanisms and determine what she really needed.

What Are the Needs?

Everyone has needs. The needs a child has in middle school are far different from the needs in elementary school. Needs of a senior in high school are far different from a ninth grader's.

Needs are determined by several things. They can be created by losses in life. (We will talk about this more in the next chapter.) They might be determined by tradition within a family or culture. The media can create needs in us we would not have otherwise. Our needs are often ingrained in us from values transferred from family and friends. Some needs—whether true or false—are passed on through generations.

One of the greatest needs I see in teens is for security. Security is the conviction of being unconditionally loved, without needing to change in order to keep that love. It is to enjoy love freely given, the kind that cannot be earned and therefore cannot be lost.

At the core of that security is the need we all have for relationships. It is built into us.

Kids strive to create friendships that validate, accept, value, and honor them.

They find companionship that gives them significance, meaning, and purpose.

Children are almost never able to articulate or even fully understand their needs, but they feel them intensely. They also choose behaviors that meet those needs. The behaviors they choose are accessible, possible, and (in their minds) effective.

When teens are caught in inappropriate behavior, I find they will stop and think when I ask, "Is this working for you?" Helping teens think about their situation and arrive at an understanding is far better than telling them what they must do, think, and believe. Their behavior is more likely to change if they come to their own conclusions about their behavior, based on their response to your question. This is far more effective than a lecture. Let them deduce what they need to. Let them recognize what is wrong about their choices. Kids are more capable of understanding their behavior than you think.

When Behavior Changes

I rarely hear kids say, "You know, my mom is not there for me." Most of the time, teens think their moms are there too much, always telling them what to do, encouraging when they need to, nagging when they have to. Moms are just there. It's in their being. Most children know it.

A child's relationship with his or her mom is like none other. Most kids believe their moms will never leave them. The connection is very special. Because most young people perceive this relationship with their moms to be so secure and so deep, they may feel more comfortable sharing deep issues with Mom than with Dad. They also feel they can express their anger (sometimes very inappropriately) to Mom because moms will take it and still be there.

Dads, on the other hand, are cool if they hang out with their kids because that is not something they tend to do. Dads can more easily make themselves absent or even walk away. As a result, when kids become teens they may not feel connected to their dads. This is especially true if the dad feels inadequate or incompetent. The result is that Dad feels hurt and withdraws when he senses a child moving away from him, or he can feel unnecessary when kids shift their attention and time from parents to peers.

When dads retreat or remove themselves from their children (or are removed from their children by divorce, death, or some other decision), problems will usually follow. Why? Because moms are the ones who instill a sense of value, and dads are the ones who validate it. All children need their fathers' "stamp of approval." When Dad's stamp of approval is not there, the child will look for validation somewhere else.

This is especially true of teenage girls. They need Dad to meet that need for validation—something only he can really fulfill. And with twelve- to fourteen-year-old girls, this need is greater than ever. Sadly, rifts between dads and daughters often occur during this time of their adolescents' lives. The results can be devastating.

Kelley

What does a girl do when Dad is not around? Some do what Kelley did. When asked about her relationship with her dad, Kelley told me the same thing I have heard a thousand times. "My dad was not there when I needed him most."

Cop-out? Excuse? Justification for inappropriate behavior? No. Catalyst in the child's mind at the time? Absolutely.

Kelley's response is typical. If I heard this from only a few girls through the years, that would be one thing. The fact that I have heard it a thousand times means to me this must be a critical factor in a young girl's life. A dad's involvement is crucial to the mental and emotional health of an adolescent and teen daughter. Dad is essential in helping her grow to maturity healthy and whole.

Let's look at Kelley's story to see what I mean. Pay special attention to this young girl's heart. You will see the goal that drove Kelley's behavior.

Like any girl, Kelley needed her dad during her early teen years. She needed affirmation, validation, direction, protection, encouragement, honor, priority, and participation. For years she had gotten these from her dad. He coached softball. He took her on trips. He left work early to spend time with her. They went to father-daughter retreats. They had father-daughter date nights. They bought each other matching pajamas for Christmas. They had tickle fights. They worked on school projects. Her dad brought special gifts to her from his business trips. She drew pictures and cut out designs for him to put on his office door.

Kelley and her dad were as close as any dad and daughter could be. In fact, they were so tight they felt a sense of loss when they were not together. There is something precious about the father-daughter relationship in the elementary school years, and Kelley and her dad had one very special relationship.

During your kids' elementary years, you transfer value to them by what you allow them to do with you. In their junior high years, you help them feel valuable by what you do with them. In their high school years, you communicate value by what you provide.

As Kelley moved into her junior high years, she felt like her Dad moved away from her. It was bad timing, because middle school girls are cruel and hateful. It's a time of awkwardness. It's a time of change. It's a time of puberty, emotions, tears, periods, bras, and new perspectives. It's a time when the exposure to life outside the confines of the home begins. Of course, hormone-laden boys enter the picture. For many girls, this is when they need their dads the most. Unfortunately, it also becomes a time when dads start to be present the least.

Some have called these years the wonder years. This is true for some parents—they wonder why they ever had kids! Other parents wonder if they should be on Valium during their child's junior high years or if they should just use duct tape and lock their kids up until adolescence passes. There is no doubt that seventh and eighth grades are tough times for youngsters. This is when kids begin to act out and start riding an emotional roller coaster.

Some people believe children are shaped most by their elementary years or their high school years, but I believe these early pre-teen and teenage years are the most important.

Personally, the things that happened in my seventh- and eighth-grade years left a mark on me. I got beaten up, moved to a new home, and discovered I had a big nose, chicken legs, and I was not as smart as I thought I was. These are still vivid memories. Ridicule, sarcasm, awkwardness, and change are all a part of the seventh- and eighth-grade package.

If Dad is not there during this time of great need, he is setting the stage for disaster. Kids' needs do not go away. They remain the same. Kids just find different ways to get those needs met.

Maybe Kelley's dad began to disappear because the sports he used to coach were now being coached by someone at the middle school or junior high. Or maybe he had a hard time making the transition from being Dad to a little girl to being Dad to a young lady. Then again, perhaps his occupation required him to work more, and time became a scarcity. Or perhaps Dad did not adjust his style of parenting in order to recognize that the concrete thinking of a young child was changing into the abstract thinking of a growing woman.

Maybe Dad had cancer treatments, and he could not be there like he used to be. Maybe he started playing golf and devoted more time to his clubs than his daughter. Maybe he decided to go back to school. Maybe Dad decided to finally deal with his alcoholism. Maybe he had an affair. Maybe he died. Maybe a divorce separated this young lady from her dad. Maybe his parents got sick, and he had to spend all his time caring for their needs.

Kelley's dad, like many dads, could have disappeared for any number of reasons. I have heard thousands of them. Some understandable, some not. Whatever the reason, Kelley felt like her dad was no longer there for her. She began to feel rejected, abandoned, lonely, and worthless. She no longer felt cherished and valued.

So the allure of a new relationship with a young man pulled her. She began to look for someone who felt the same as she did, who understood, who made her feel important, and came alongside her in her struggle to fill the void left by an absent dad. Kelley's needs remained the same. Her goal was to meet those needs. Her behavior changed to reach that goal.

Kelley began to hang out with a new group of kids, especially one young man she stated, "is a lot like my dad." As her friendship grew with this fifteen-year-old kid, so did their physical relationship. At fifteen, Kelley became pregnant.

She was the star cheerleader at her school, and her friends gathered around her and adopted her as their new project. She became a novelty, a pregnant glamor girl everyone adored. Youth ministers invited her to come talk to their youth group about the evils of a sexual relationship. Inside, Kelley was struggling. Struggling so much that she began to smoke pot.

I find that most people who smoke dope are trying to combat their own depression … an observation based on forty years of spending time with kids who smoke pot. It is one of the hardest habits for kids to break, one of the most damaging drugs with long-term consequences.

On the nights when Kelley was not smoking, she was drinking. And she was still sexually active. Kelley was a young girl in deep pain. Unbelievably, most people thought she had it all together. In reality, she was a mess. Her actions were not working for her.

She gave birth to a little girl. Kelley's parents decided to raise the baby, while Kelley secretly continued her addictive habits to combat her internal pain and confusion. One day she was arrested with enough dope to choke a horse. All of a sudden, Kelley's hidden actions were exposed, and her world came crashing down around her.

The community that supported her as she wrestled through her pregnancy now began to reject and shun the one they formerly embraced. The emotional roller coaster became too hard for Kelley to bear. The young girl who was once the pride of the town was now a pathetic mess of a teen who really just wanted to have her dad around.

I wonder sometimes if the reason dads get so mad at the young men who steal their daughters is that they are reminded of all they have not done. They see how they have failed with their daughters.

What If You Can't Determine the Needs?

Most parents say they understand the model I described and agree that all behavior is driven by some goal. They look at Ashley's and Kelley's bad behavior and agree these two young ladies had reasons for their actions. They even agree with me it is no surprise the girls are messed up.

Then they add, "But what about my child? We don't see any losses, cannot determine what her needs are, and cannot put our finger on the real issues!"

Unfortunately, sometimes a child's behavior defies explanation. I see situations where no cause-and-effect equation or logical pattern or identified loss is evident. Sometimes behavior cannot be categorized as rebellion.

In these situations, time will usually expose the motives and goals behind the behavior. All you can do is make every effort to stop inappropriate behavior and hope one day your child will process what he or she is doing and come to some conclusions.

Even when you cannot explain kids' behavior, my encouragement to all parents is not to disengage from your children when your kids need you the most. If you abandon children during a time of difficulty or bad behavior, who will help them process the way they think about who they are? In difficult times, parents and children tend to withdraw. Kids' withdrawal is based on shame and guilt. Your withdrawal may be because of the pain or shame their behavior is causing. Perhaps you disengage because you don't understand what is going on. But if you pull out emotionally during this time, how will your kids ever learn about God's grace, His acceptance, or His love when they don't feel lovely? J.R.R. Tolkien once said, "Faithless is he that says farewell when the road darkens."[1]

When You Unknowingly Cause Some of Your Teen's Behavior

These next few paragraphs could easily be turned into a whole book. I am convinced all parents do things that bug our kids. Many times we do things or don't do things that ignite and fuel their anger. Left unresolved and not discussed, parents provoke their children. They do not put their efforts into determining the cause of behavior and the motivation for it because they are so busy trying to stop the inappropriate behavior.

I mentioned in a previous chapter that all behavior is goal-oriented. Kids do things to fulfill a perceived need in their life, and sometimes do them in a way that violates every value, principle, and standard parents work hard to build into their lives.

From my experience, the seriousness of the inappropriate behavior a child displays (and most times hides) is not necessarily a sign of the intensity of their rebellion. Rather, it shows the depth of their need and the driving force behind their behavior. It's usually an issue of the heart. That being said, you can spend all the time you want changing the behavior, but you will never get to the real issue until you help a teen resolve their motives for the behavior. The kids who come to our Heartlight residential counseling center get there because of their behavior. But behavior is not the real issue. The real issue is what's going on in their hearts. Once we go to the source of the issue, the behavior usually corrects itself.

Here are a couple of examples of how dads and moms have been the source of the problem without realizing it. Their teen felt a void he tried to fill with inappropriate behavior. Please focus on the process of how a teen responds to the actions of parents.

Dads, let me give you an example first.

Let's say Dad gets angry pretty easily. The anger is probably motivated by a desire for good things for his kids, but when good things are not happening, Dad gets angry and starts to yell. He lets everyone know how disappointed he is. The son then feels like he can never please his Dad. The son tries to avoid any situation where Dad is upset in order to steer clear of conflict. He moves away from the relationship with his dad that he desperately wants and needs. The son cannot see his need for his dad, because Dad's angry diatribes get in the way of how the son sees him.

The son feels devalued, hates Dad's authoritarian approach, believes he can't measure up, feels the loss of a dad who used to be his hero (and whose flaws he now clearly sees), and begins to think he is a failure.

To cope with all these feeling and emotions, the son decides to dull his pain with alcohol and pot. He begins to hang around other "bad kids" who make him feel welcome, and he gives up all academic and athletic pursuits because he has now found the place of rest always longed for with a group of unmotivated kids striving for nothing. He bonds with kids who love things he once used to hate.

The behavior is inappropriate, but the heart of the matter is not the son's actions. Those are merely symptoms of a greater issue: the loss of his relationship with his dad (unintentional on his part).

Dad, this is where it is important to look at the plank of your own before you stare at the speck in the eye of your son. From my experience living with hundreds of young men, I am convinced the wrath of a father never moves a teen to repentance and positive behavioral change. While a dad might feel more powerful when he exercises his right to display his anger, he does not get the message across he hopes his fireworks display will convey.

Dads, here is a Scripture for you. It is 1 Corinthians 16:13, and it says, "Be on your guard, stand firm in the faith, be courageous, be strong. Do everything in love." Watch out for your kids, hold to the standards and biblical principles, and do not walk away from what you hold to be true for your family. Be strong. Stand for what is right. However, do not forget that last charge Paul gives us here, "Do everything in love." Let that, not your anger, be the way you approach your kids. It is hard to hear someone yell and scream at you and feel like that is an expression of love.

Moms, it's your turn. You have the amazing ability to want the best for your kids always. It is hard for you to get that off your mind. You are wired that way. However, your constant correction feels like incessant nagging. Your efforts to help your kids do their best feel like telling them they do everything wrong. When you keep telling your daughter what she needs to do differently, she may respond by staying far away from you. Your son too!

Your intentions are good. You want your kids to strive to be their best, to do a little better all the time. However, it starts to feel like a critical spirit that is dragging them down. Instead of seeing themselves as precious in your eyes, now they see themselves as flawed.

Your daughter begins to hear, over and over and over, that she is broken, that something is wrong with her, that she can do no right, that she is not appreciated, that she has to be perfect, and that she will never measure up. She sees no relief in sight. Your son begins to feel that he is not good enough, that you always want more, that nothing he does is enough.

Then behavior starts to change. Kids begin rolling their eyes, progress to verbally "mouthing off," then intensely challenge, perhaps yell when they can't get their point across. Your wonderful relationship deteriorates into a confused "What's happening here?" mess.

To find a place of rest, a daughter may find a young man who listens and does not criticize her. Your daughter begins to give in to anything he says he needs in order to have a relationship where she feels wanted, loved, and accepted, faults and all. A son may rebel in other ways, or he may also find company with a young lady who makes him feel respected and loved.

The kids' behavior is inappropriate. But the real problem is the loss they feel in their relationship with their mother, the one who used to love them so dearly and receive their love freely in return. The source of the issue is not their behavior; it is the negativity they feel from their well-meaning mom, who truly wants only the best for her children.

Moms, here's a Scripture I hope you will hide in your heart. Ephesians 4:29 says, "Do not let any unwholesome talk come out of your mouths, but only what is helpful for building others up according to their needs, that it may benefit all who listen."

Why do your children do the things they do? There might be a million reasons. As a fellow parent, I implore you to make sure you are not the cause. If you think you are, make adjustments so your children can once again see their preciousness in your eyes. Bad behavior will usually change when value and honor are restored. Make sure you resolve these issues, so your children have the best chance to change.

Is My Child Wired Differently?

Some kids' behavior can only be explained by the fact that they are just wired differently. These kids have no particular crisis or trauma that moves them toward bad behavior. Nor do they have some remarkable need a parent would notice. It is just the way they behave.

I divide these young people into two groups. The first are those who might have what I call silent issues. These issues are usually invisible until they are reflected in kids' screaming behavior. This behavior many times is misdiagnosed, and the children are labeled rebellious, obstinate, belligerent, selfish, stubborn, or strong-willed.

The correct diagnosis might be attention deficit disorder, personality disorder, obsessive-compulsive disorder, logic sequence problems, intelligence or emotional challenges, or learning disabilities. I am not a psychiatrist or a psychologist. I cannot diagnose these things, but I have been around young people who have these behavior issues enough to realize how often kids are misdiagnosed.

Dan

Dan came to us as a seventeen-year-old who was flunking out of school. He related to people inappropriately, used drugs, sneaked away from home at night, and did anything he could to ignore his parents' wishes.

After Dan arrived at Heartlight, we saw he actually wanted to stop and think before he acted, but he couldn't. He wanted to get help in counseling, but he just could not connect the dots. He wanted to be socially acceptable, but he could not make it happen. As time passed, we found Dan could only read at a second-grade level, had a very low IQ, and suffered from learning disabilities and a logic sequence problem.

For whatever reason, Dan's parents and teachers never saw these problems and interpreted his behavior as an attitude problem coupled with rebellion and anger. They did not know. The effects of not knowing caused amazing damage.

Dan's parents had to adjust their hopes for their child. He was not going to be a brain surgeon. He was not going to go to college. He would need to choose an occupation where he could use his hands. Their response to his inadequacies began to change when they realized they misunderstood his issues.

By the way, I find some families do not want to accept who their child is or recognize their child's future is not going to be what they thought it was. Dan's parents wanted Dan's problems to be rebellion, an apathetic attitude, and anger because those things can change. It was more difficult for them to accept Dan had deficits that might remain for a lifetime. Their eventual acceptance of their son's true diagnoses changed Dan's behavior. The pressure was off, and they lowered their expectations to an acceptable and achievable level.

Dan was no longer frustrated for not being where everyone else seemed to think he needed to be. He was no longer angry for not getting what he wanted. What he thought he wanted was really what everyone else wanted for him, things he could never achieve.

Finally, Dan's rebellion ceased. When Dan and his parents accepted his limitations, he began to live as a real person, not some virtual person who was never going to live up to the fantasy placed on him by his parents. His parents finally realized he was acting inappropriately because he could not fulfill their expectations.

Other Idiosyncrasies

The second group of young people who are wired differently are those born with either low self-image, a need for thrills or excitement, a strong creative bent, or other unique tendencies. They are made that way, and chances are they will always be that way. You can try all you want, but these kids will not change because they can't. In these cases, parents need to learn to appreciate the uniqueness of their children. They must find the treasure in their children's hearts and rejoice in the way God created them.

Curiosity vs. Goal-Oriented Behavior

The Internet is a useful tool. What it offers to all of us is amazing. But what it exposes our children to can be so damaging. I am not just talking about sexualized sites and pornography. I am talking about exposure to the bizarre and the corruptive. A bad combination of availability and curiosity can sometimes have deadly results.

A few years ago I had never heard of cutting, a form of self-injury. I had never heard of the choking game, also called "space monkey." In this form of entertainment, people choke themselves, depriving their brain of oxygen momentarily, to achieve a euphoric drug-like high. I did not know anorexia would become the new diet. Or that huffing certain inhalants around the house would allow kids to get high and overcome their boredom.

Young people are curious. Through the Internet they are encouraged to experiment out of intrigue and fascination. Because it is available and kids hear about it, they try it. They may have a reason behind their behavior, but most likely not. It is not about sex, drugs, or alcohol. These are just ways of being curious without committing other sins.

Will there be new temptations in the future? Absolutely. Will they entice our kids to wrong behavior? You bet. The motive behind the behavior? To quote President Clinton, "I did it, because I could."[2]

Normal but Inappropriate Behavior

A man recently told me his son has a problem with pornography. As we talked, he stated that his son came to him feeling guilty because he was on the Internet and saw some things that were inappropriate.

Is viewing pornography inappropriate? Yes. Did the son have a problem with pornography? Perhaps not. It may have been just an issue of availability. It was simply too accessible. A woman is one of God's most beautiful creations. God created man with a desire to enjoy a woman's beauty. A man's longing for a woman is normal. Fulfilling sexual longing outside of marriage is inappropriate. Period. So is indulging in fantasies with graphic images. When you see this type of behavior, it may simply be an availability issue. Solve the availability problem (monitor the Internet), and the behavior will take care of itself.

Now What?

As we have seen, behaviors can spring from various causes. Regardless of the reason for inappropriate behavior, any child can learn to be obedient, respectful, and honest. All kids can learn not to do things as easily as they learn to do them. Understanding the source of your child's behaviors helps you choose the right approach for tackling those behaviors. For any of these issues, immaturity calls for boundaries, rebellion calls for consequences, and some behaviors call for restrictions.

Remember, most behavior has a motive or at least a reason. The motives and reasons should be the focus of your correction. The behavior is not the issue. It may be the presenting problem and need to be corrected, but wise parents look also to the cause of the behavior. They help children learn that inappropriate behavior is not getting them to the place they want to be.

Look with the eyes of your heart to see what is behind your child's behavior. Your child may not say it, but he will appreciate your effort to find the root of the problem and help him change his life.

CHAPTER SEVEN

THE IMPORTANCE OF PAIN

*C*rushed to the airport, determined to get settled in plenty of time to start writing this chapter. I planned my trip home so I could have the full day to work on it. I even saved a couple hundred dollars by purchasing a ticket that would allow another stop, another plane, and an extra few hours of travel so I would have plenty of time to write. My plans were to get settled early, grab a hot latte, and begin the task of writing a chapter on pain. Little did I know what was ahead.

As I went through airport security, I followed the usual routine of unbuckling my belt, taking off my watch, removing my computer from my bag, and pulling off my boots. I placed everything on the conveyer belt to have the items scanned. As I was standing in line, the lady behind me was doing the same thing. When she pulled out her laptop, it fell out of her hands and headed to the floor. Her clumsiness was about to change my plans for the day.

About that time, everything started to go in slow motion. I watched in disbelief as I realized—much too late—the computer was headed straight for my foot. Before I could react, it nailed my big toe right at the base of my toenail.

When it hit, I felt as if someone cut my toe off. The pain raced to my head. I broke out in a sweat, and I kicked her computer like a hockey puck across the floor as angry thoughts and waves of pain overwhelmed me. I started feeling faint.

I hobbled with all my stuff to a seat with and pulled off my sock to find that my toenail had already pulled away from my toe. The pressure underneath the nail continued to build. It was so red it looked like someone hammered it. That laptop did.

I thought I could walk it off and put it out of my mind. Instead, the pain increased. I still ordered my latte—sweating and hoping for some relief. I took a sip, but the pain was so great, it did not taste right. I threw it away and hobbled to my gate, barely able to think about anything but the pain shooting through my foot.

I got on the plane, and as we took off, I sat praying for a miracle and trying not to swear out loud. The pain just got worse. I could barely sit still. I thought, *How can a toe hurt so much?* I silently cussed and held back the tears. I drank three little bottles of vodka. I did not care about anyone around me. I thought only about myself. I smiled at no one and ignored everything. Quite honestly, I was writhing in such pain I really did not care if the plane crashed. I could not sleep, thought dark thoughts, and felt bitter toward that stupid woman who could not control her own laptop.

That is when it hit me: Pain changed me. Then I thought, "God just allowed a wonderful introduction to this chapter on pain."

By the time I finally arrived in Dallas, the Advil (and other things) began to work. And by the time I got home—some nine hours after I left Chicago—my toe was still uncomfortable, but it was tolerable.

The Power of Pain

I was amazed where the pain had taken me. It impacted every part of my life. It changed my attitude. I was short with people, and the day became very, very long.

Things that should have been funny were not. I was angry instead of happy. Because I was experiencing such severe pain, I could not stay focused. I was jumpy. I was hyper. From the moment the pain hit, nothing was enjoyable. Food did not taste good, coffee tasted worse, and my appetite was replaced by a gut ache. Important calls, schedules, and conversations were no longer foremost on my mind. The only thing that became important was relief from my pain. It became my focus, my purpose, and my sole desire.

I wonder if most inappropriate behavior is an attempt to stop pain. I could not help but notice that many of my responses to pain were no different than what I see in the lives of teens around me.

What Pain Produces

We all endure times of intense pain. Perhaps you are there right now. Or maybe someone around you—your child—is showing the same symptoms I had.

Pain usually produces the same response in all of us. What was once important becomes irrelevant. The pain itself overwhelms every part of life, and we are focused on finding relief. My own pain produced some things in me that are not part of my normal makeup. For instance, my pain made me more sensitive to others. I noticed hurting people more than I noticed them before. People with hurt feet, on crutches, in wheelchairs, limping. I also slowed down. I asked for help (something I don't usually do).

My pain also taught me a few things. First, it taught me to watch out for flying laptops. Second, I learned to keep my boots on as long as I could. Third, I am more careful to make sure I do not injure someone else the way I was injured. Most of all, I learned that most people operate differently in pain. Maybe some of their behavior is a result of the pain they are experiencing.

Embracing Pain

When we are in pain, we think the pain is going to last forever. Yet most pain in our lives is temporary. Remember 2 Corinthians 4:17? It reminds us pain is not only temporary but also has an incredible outcome: "For our light and momentary troubles are achieving for us an eternal glory that far outweighs them all" (NIV).

C.S. Lewis states, "God whispers to us in our pleasures, speaks in our conscience, but shouts in our pains: It is His megaphone to rouse a deaf world."[1] Pain is an instrument He uses to expose who we really are and how life really is, and to bring us to a place in life where we seek Him for answers. We all desire to run from pain, but it is a tool that causes us to question our current circumstances and reevaluate our goals and motives.

Avoiding pain in your own life—or the life of your child—allows childish thinking and foolish behavior to continue. That can result in greater pain.

I don't know any parents who enjoy watching their children go through painful times. Everything in us wants to bail our children out of their pain and keep them from hurting. But God continues to show me that pain is an instrument He uses—and perhaps at times even causes—to motivate us to move to a new level of personal and spiritual maturity.

The Value of Pain

I learned God uses pain to develop sensitivity in us and help us grow. I realize now that by trying to avoid pain, I sometimes get in the way of God's plan, preventing Him from molding me and the people I love into the people He desires us to be. As hard as it is to admit, my well-intentioned actions, at times, preclude God's work in people's lives.

I learned our attempt to lessen our children's pain only postpones the inevitable. When we succeed, the suffering comes back at a later date when the consequences of choices are greater. Let me give you an example.

I have always been a supporter of homeschooling. I still am. Please don't dog me for my homeschool comments. We homeschool all of the sixty kids at Heartlight at any given time. For all the good reasons, I think homeschooling is truly a great idea. So do not read into this example that I am against homeschooling. But I do have some concerns about how, through homeschooling, we can overprotect our children. Under our supervision and shelter, kids may not have to develop some of the critical decision-making skills to help them later in life.

Homeschooling does protect. That is not the problem. However, in some instances, homeschooling does not allow kids to be exposed (a little bit at a time) to a pain-filled world bent on their destruction. Parents become overly protective because they know the hardships kids face "out there." They do not want their kids to experience pain.

As a result, children grow up in a painless environment and fail to develop decision-making skills in tough situations. Kids need to learn how to share, how to handle conflict, how to make choices, how to walk away from dangerous situations, how to operate in social settings, how to fit in, how to function as maturing adults, and how to behave appropriately when everything around them is inappropriate.

As parents, you and I certainly want to protect our children. But we must also *prepare* our children. By preventing pain, we let our children live in a bubble that can carry them to their destruction. Our well-intended insulation and isolation of our children can bring about unintended, devastating results.

Allowing a child to experience pain is difficult. For example, the same sympathetic heart that moves a parent to adopt a child may be motivated keep the child from experiencing further pain. The same generosity that drives you to provide for your child can keep your child from learning how to live without some things.

Your desire to protect can prevent your child from struggling through the process of discovery.

We parents must see that momentary pain motivates our children to reconsider options, reflect on choices, and reevaluate where their current choices have placed them. A child will only touch a hot stove once. But kids today are not allowed to touch that hot stove. Matter of fact, many are not even allowed in the kitchen because Mom (or Dad) is doing all the cookin'. Parents often control things, and control them tightly.

That kind of control and overprotection is detrimental to a child's development. Mom and Dad, understand that experience is a good teacher. Allowing a child to fail is sometimes a good thing. Permitting a child to feel emotional hurt and even some physical pain can do some pretty good things for that child.

You know, I think I would brush and floss my teeth a whole lot more if my dentist did not use Novocain to deaden the pain of drilling when she fills my cavities. I would do what I needed to avoid that pain. Pain is a powerful motivator.

Can Sitting in Jail Be a Good Thing?

A few years ago, a father named Bill called me on Christmas Eve and asked for a few minutes of my time. I could tell he was desperate, angry, and hurt just by the trembling in his voice.

After a warm greeting, he began to tell me his son Brian was arrested for possession of narcotics, resisting arrest, and driving under the influence. Now Brian sat in a jail cell in Seattle.

Bill's family was supposed to go to Colorado the next day for a skiing vacation with the extended family. It was their vacation of a lifetime, one they planned for a long time and anticipated for months.

Bill told me he could bail out his son, and the son could join the family on the trip; but Bill was having second thoughts about rescuing his son. He did not know what would be best. Was it better to bail his son out of jail and take him on the trip (After all, it was Christmas.)? Or leave him to spend the next ten days in jail while the family was off enjoying their time together on this long-awaited vacation? This loving father did not know whether he should endure the pain of not having his son on the trip and allow his son to experience the pain of his choices. Or if he should come to the rescue, call it "grace," and bail the son out to join them, casting a shadow of tension over the family trip. Tough decision.

Brian was raised in a home where he was given everything, had to work for little, and was pretty much enabled to do just about anything he wanted to do. I knew from previous conversations that his dad was always bailing him out of things. Brian never had to pay the price for anything. Dad always rescued.

Call it what you want, but this young man had been enabled, permitted, and allowed to continue in his foolish thinking and crazy behavior, never touching the hot stove of life. He never experienced the pain that would correct his thinking and steer him toward good choices.

I told Bill to let him sit. I encouraged this poor dad to see now was the time for him to stop rescuing his son and allow Brian to pay the price for his poor and immature choices. It would be a lesson Brian would not forget, and one that would not come easy. But it was time. Taking a stand now might save Brian's life in the long run.

Quite honestly, I did not think Bill would take my suggestion or listen to my advice. But when I called Bill in Colorado a few days later and asked him how things were going on their vacation, he tearfully said it was miserable. Brian was still in jail, and Bill admitted it was hard to enjoy his vacation knowing where his son was spending Christmas. Still, Bill went on to say he knew the decision to have Brian sit tight was the right one.

Personally, I think the whole process was really more about Bill than Brian. Frankly, the whole family was elated Dad finally stood up to his son and chose not to enable his son's antics any more. Bill finally realized he was empowering his son to live a lifestyle that could eventually lead to his premature death.

As hard as it was for Brian's dad to leave him in that jail cell, and as tough as it was for Brian to stay there, it ended up being one of the greatest weeks in Brian's life. That week everything came crashing down. For the first time, Brian knew broken-ness. For someone who thought he always had it all together, the experience was profound.

In his brokenness, Brian made a commitment to Christ—a commitment rooted in a deep understanding of his need for a Savior. In fact, after Brian was released from jail, he commemorated his transformation with a tattoo across the underside of his arm, where these beautiful words appear: "If the Son sets you free, you will be free indeed" (John 8:36).

Brian's dad finally allowed pain to take full effect on his son. The result? Brian's life was transformed. The only thing I wonder is whether Brian would have gotten there sooner if his dad had not bailed him out so much. As I think about Brian's story, Proverbs 19:18 (NIV) comes to mind: "Discipline your children, for in that there is hope; do not be a willing party to their death."

I believe God is encouraging us as parents to allow pain in our children's lives to help set the boundaries of choices, and to let consequences have their full impact. This helps our children recognize and heed the warning signs when tough situations come: Don't go there.

Rescuing Can Make Things Worse

Parents are wired to protect their children. It's natural. However, parents are also wired to prepare their children. Unfortunately, our generation focuses more on protection than it does preparation, which is why many teens today are so immature.

Many times, teens don't grow up because we don't let them. Even though most teens are capable of acting as adults, intellectually and biologically, our well-meaning actions shelter, confine, control, and anesthetize our children from the hardships vital to their growth. Our actions, restrictions, and limits do not prepare. Sometimes, they hinder.

Let me give you some scenarios I believe can inhibit you from preparing your child for his or her future. These are scenarios I see play out repeatedly, hurting a child instead of helping.

1. Parents ignore the low performance of their children. They constantly complain about the teachers. They are reluctant to accept the fact their children may have a low IQ or academic problem.

2. Mom and Dad rescue their son every time he gets in trouble at school, saying he is just "all boy." As a result, they postpone the consequences for inappropriate behavior by allowing their son's childish behavior to continue far too long.

3. Dad fears confronting a daughter who treats her mother terribly. He thinks if he demands respect in his home,

she will run away. She ends up ruining relationships with family members and leaves anyway.

4. Parents are afraid to set rules and boundaries within their home. They know the children won't like the new policies, and they want to avoid conflict.

5. A father bails his child out of speeding tickets and personally pays the insurance rate hikes. Rather than grounding the son from using the car, he empowers him to continue his reckless behavior, and the son finally kills someone.

6. Parents do not let their children handle their own money, fearing they might bounce a check or misuse the funds. Kids never learn how to handle finances. When they get married, the marriage falls apart because of financial mismanagement.

7. Mom is afraid to follow through on the consequences for her kids' behavior. She does not stay strong and is not confident in that role.

8. A mom bails a child out of jail because she does not want her daughter to be around the inmates. Her own pain at the thought of her child spending the night in jail or detention prevents the daughter from experiencing the pain necessary to stop the behavior that got her there. (By the way, your child will probably learn the lesson the first time if you remain strong, and she will ultimately bless you for doing what was needed at such a critical time.)

9. Parents are afraid to accept the fact that their children are spinning out of control for fear they might look bad in the community. (Most kids eventually nosedive in such a case, and the whole community is keenly aware of the failure.)

10. Mom and Dad never say no.

11. Parents do not get help for children who struggle socially until the children's relationships are terribly damaged.

12. Mom cannot believe her son would "do such a thing," so she sweeps his behavior under the rug, only to have it crawl back into the light when the local police knock on the front door.

13. Parents do not stand up for what they believe for fear of their son's response. They wonder why their child does not stand up for what he believes with his friends.

These are a few examples. There are many more. The common thread? Overprotection or fear of conflict with teens. Many times, parents' fear prevents them from walking with their children through difficult times or times of pain. When a teen makes a pretty serious blunder, parents should never ignore the situation. Two wrongs do not make a right. When children are wrong, parents need to do what is right.

Parents, be strong. Stand up to your teens. Yes, it's tough. It's unpleasant. It's no fun. But it's far better than facing bail bondsmen and planning funerals.

Other Ways We Rescue our Kids

I travel quite a bit, as many as two hundred days a year. I have accumulated more than five million miles on my favorite carrier, American Airlines. I know airports, the tricks of travel, and feel comfortable living out of a suitcase.

When I am home in Texas, I live with sixty high school kids at a time at Heartlight. Twenty-five guys and thirty-five young ladies from all over the country who are struggling. Recently, I just happened to be traveling the same day a few of our girls were traveling. (Okay, maybe it didn't just happen. Actually, I plan my schedule that way so I can help kids negotiate the Dallas airport.)

Anyway, I was on this trip and had four of our seventeen- to eighteen-year-old girls on my flight to Dallas. Upon arrival, the girls were not sure how to ride the tram, get to their next gate, and make their connecting flight. I helped them all. One of the girls made a comment that stuck with me: "If you weren't here, I think I would have been lost and never gotten home."

My first thought was to wonder how this seventeen-year-old could have felt lost, when she has traveled more than any young lady I know. Then it hit me. When she traveled in the past, she never had to think. She had no opportunities to figure anything out on her own. Mom or Dad did all her thinking. In addition, she said she had never traveled alone. When our Heartlight teens go home on a plane for a break, they always travel without adults. It gives them responsibility, shows our trust in them, and teaches them to operate in the world without supervision.

When Moms and Dads fail to start handing over the reins of control to adolescents, by the time kids are in the their upper teens and getting close to adulthood, they are not ready. Keeping kids powerless cripples them from growing up to be capable adults. Sometimes, they can't even get through an airport. We rescue when we do not allow our teens to learn new things, for fear they might make a wrong or bad decision.

Another way parents rescue their teens is by feeling the need to constantly amuse and entertain them. Life is not always fun. It is often a lot of work. To entertain kids all the time is to set them up for disappointment when it is time to be an adult. One young man I know pretty much thinks most of life is "boring" when Mom and Dad are not playing the role of entertainment directors aboard the "family cruise ship."

His parents believe their son will get in trouble if he has idle time, so they fill his days with fun. It is not working. The son needs bigger and better thrills, because too much fun takes the fun out of everything. It's a paradox, I know. But too much of anything turns bad. Now the son pursues anything he can to get a thrill out of every second of his life.

I wonder what he is going to do when life is not so thrilling, when his marriage is not one big honeymoon, and when his own kids one day struggle. Mom and Dad prevent this child from knowing what real life is like. He does not know how to work, how to submit to another's authority, or fulfill normal expectations.

Sometimes, I see parents rescue their teens from the pain of life by excusing certain inappropriate and unacceptable behaviors. One time, Jan and I were eating dinner with one of the girls at Heartlight. As we talked and ate, her comments about others, including her family members and friends, became overtly rude, harsh, abrasive, and disrespectful. She felt free to talk that way because Mom and Dad did not teach her how to treat others with respect.

Instead of accepting a principal's comments about a child's disrespect and inappropriate actions, or a youth minister's concerns about dishonesty and unacceptable comments made at youth group, I see Dads defend their daughters because they have a desperate need to be the "knight in shining armor." In this case, the daughter quickly learns Dad rescues her from pain. His need to be her hero does not allow the daughter to develop honesty and integrity. When this girl is an adult, others will not rescue like Dad will. Her relationships are likely to suffer.

Facing the Pain

Pain will come as children mature and start to take on their own identities. Watching children mature can be painful. They will make bad choices as they strive for independence. This is a critical component of growing up prepared for healthy adulthood. For the most part, parents are not doing a good job of allowing kids to experience and learn from mistakes if they continue to protect their teens as much as they did when those teens were toddlers.

Here is another example. I am all for every kid on the team getting a trophy when they are in the first few grades of their elementary years. However, to give trophies to each team in eighth grade, even the teams that did not win, does not help prepare kids for what high school will be like. The sting of losing is an appropriate pain to allow your kids to feel. Parents, you also need to quit avoiding your own pain. It will hurt to see your child lose. It hurts to see your kid hurt. But pain is important. Pain causes growth. Conflict creates change.

Suffer the small hurts as your child grows, so the big hurts don't come later as a result of your overprotection.

Pain comes when you begin to have difficult conversations with your daughter about values. You hurt if you realize she is not on the same page as you in moral and ethical areas. But she needs you to face and handle these painful discussions. If you disengage from her during this time, who is going to help her formulate or reset her values?

Pain comes when you confront foolish thinking—yours or your child's. No parents like to have their foolish ways or thinking exposed. No kids like having their foolish thinking uncovered. You still have to face it. Lovingly confront your children, and be open to their criticism of you.

Pain comes when you and your son have conflicting ideas, when you don't agree on his relationships, when you expose his motives, or when he exposes yours.

Pain comes when you confront your kids regarding behaviors that are out of line or just wrong. These discussions may get a little heated. If you can't stand the heat, I encourage you to turn down the temperature a little bit. Take a small break, and then get back together to discuss things further.

By the way, I am amazed at how fearful most parents are about anger and the expression of it. Scripture assures us we can be angry and not sin. Anger can be good. The intensity of our anger can reflect the longings of our heart for something good in the lives of our kids.

Pain comes when parents function as goalkeepers. The goalkeeper is the one who has to constantly point toward a goal and say, "Yes, this is the way we're headed," or "No, this is not the way we're going." Both those statements can be painful.

Pain comes when your daughter begins her quest for independence. Let me encourage you not to confuse this desire for independence with selfishness. You want your daughter to be independent when she leaves home and goes off to school or work. But independence comes at a price.

None of us enjoys these times of pain, but they are opportunities to guide and steer your child through rough waters when the guidance and steering are needed the most. Don't bail out when the going gets rough. Put on your armor (Ephesians 6:10-17) and go to battle for the heart, mind, and spirit of your children.

You and your child will receive cuts, bruises, knicks, and wounds. But battle scars are better than potentially fatal wounds that come when a soldier is left stranded to face the enemy. Parents, surround your child on the battlefield of life. Allow him to fight his own battles. Just make sure you are there to get his back.

Dads and Pain

Avoiding pain is easy, especially for us dads. We are great at checking out. I see dad after dad who boils, stews, and allows unresolved issues to destroy his relationship with his children. Or who avoids conflict by compromising his standards. Then there are the dads who cover up problems by overindulging their kids, creating a deflection from the problem and causing even more problems.

Dads, you can choose to ignore what is really happening with your children and steer clear of the painful experience of dealing with the issues. But by ignoring or avoiding situations that cause pain, you miss incredible opportunities to move your child *through* the pain. Moving through the pain produces character that not be developed any other way. When you sidestep painful situations in your child's life, you are allowing his or her immaturity and foolish thinking to continue.

Dads, do what is right, regardless of your feelings. Do not wait until you feel like the moment is right. It will never feel right. Remember, parenting is not about you; it is about helping your child develop into a moral, loving man or woman who can function in the world with healthy relationships and a productive life.

The Other Side of Pain

Pain has an amazing way of bringing about maturity. The young people who come to live with us in our residential program at Heartlight are often very mature. They are young men and women forced to struggle through the difficult and painful issues of death, divorce, victimization, and hurt. They have issues they have yet to resolve, but they do have a maturity about them because of the pain of their circumstances.

Growing Your Child Through Pain

Parents who recognize the value of pain and conflict begin to see struggles in a new light. They begin to understand their children are seeking answers in life, so the parents embrace the pain and struggles as opportunities to move their children toward a deeper understanding of their need for a Savior. They do not provide all the answers to their children's searching; they provide direction.

If parents always give searching children the answers, rather than allowing them to work through their questions, the children may lose their motivation to continue seeking. On the other hand, when parents remain engaged and give direction without always giving answers, they encourage their kids to keep searching. When a child begins to seek on his own, he finds.

Pain and discomfort motivate. In fact, your teens will continue in their behavior until the pain that is a result of behavior is greater than the pleasure derived from it. Pain also teaches. For example, kids in pain frequently develop empathy and sympathy toward others who are hurting. They are able to make connections with those in pain. Because they feel deeply, they relate to others who hurt.

Of course, we should not cause pain in our children's lives. But an appropriate level of discomfort will help our children move away from a place they don't want to be. The key for parents is to remain engaged when their children go through pain. Be available to give some good guidance and clear options.

Kids in Pain

Young people in pain do not always make good decisions. Shoot, they don't make good decisions when they aren't in pain! Be understanding. Find out what is bothering your child. As you do, you begin to move toward your child when she is in pain. She needs you to walk with her through difficult times.

By the way, young people in pain will sometimes appear to be more selfish than those who are not. Even when they experience grace, they may not accept it as such. They are so set on self-preservation they often would not be able to see grace if it bit them on the nose! Remember, when teens are acting out, they may just be trying to get out of their pain. Their choices are usually designed to help them find relief from their pain. Pain causes people to do things they would not normally do. Wise parents are there to help guide their kids even when times are ugly. God is at work in their lives, and we don't want to impede His process.

Please hear me on this: Pain never justifies a person's inappropriate behavior. However, understanding your child's pain helps you know how to help. Yes, you must hold the line. Sometimes a tight grip hurts; other times, a firm grip gives your child a sense of security.

Know when to hold tight and when a loose hug will make all the difference in the world.

The moment you and your child experience pain may not be the moment you have to move. When your child acts inappropriately, you might want to stand back, evaluate, give it some time (perhaps twenty-four hours), and then determine what to do. Decide whether the pain your child is going through is enough to teach him or her the lesson that's needed. Natural consequences, rather than enforced consequences, often do the trick.

One more time, Mom and Dad, quit rescuing your teen from pain now. You are only postponing the pain to a later time in life when the hurt is greater, lessons are harder, and consequences affect a greater number of people.

CHAPTER EIGHT

Losses Behind Behaviors

*W*hen Jan and I had been married for some years, I was stunned at her announcement one day. I thought I knew everything about my wife, but she surprised me when she said she wanted to see a counselor. I knew Jan and her history, but I did not know the depth of the pain she still felt. Like a typical male, I had no idea what she was talking about.

Tearfully, Jan began to explain the sense of loss she felt from the sexual abuse she experienced as a child. She realized she needed to deal with that loss. She was worn out from her constant attempts to manage the feelings and hurts from years earlier. I realized my wife could no longer live with the unresolved issues surrounding her abuse. She was fighting depression, had relational issues in her family that no one had dealt with (and everyone quietly avoided), and she felt unsettled in her head and heart.

We started to go to counseling. We made the decision for her sake, but it soon became an opportunity for both of us. As I watched the counselor gently peel back the layers of emotion in Jan's life, I began to see how her loss played such an integral role in her existence and in our relationship. The counseling process lasted eighteen months. We drove two hours each way to spend two hours with a counselor. I loved that time and hated it.

I loved learning how we were wired differently and how various things in our lives molded our thinking, behaviors, and interactions with others. I hated the pain that came out of it, for Jan and for me, individually and as a couple. I learned so many things, including the way we handle loss by filling the emptiness with things that do not last. Jan's recognition of the futility of her efforts to fill those voids moved her to a desperate point of pain, causing her to question her current state and long for something different.

In my years of work with struggling teens and their families, I have seen this same thing over and over in young ladies who were sexually abused. Let me give you an example of what I am talking about.

Anna

Anna was sexually abused by her grandfather for years. It started at age two and lasted until a seventh-grade slumber party, when one of Anna's friends heard her innocently share what her grandfather was doing to her. This sweet little friend told Anna she should tell her mother. She did, and that was it. At least for a while.

As Anna matured, she began to understand more fully the violation of her body during those earlier years. The older she got, the more furious she became. She exerted more and more effort to counteract the damage her grandfather caused in her. She wore herself out trying to prove to herself he had no more control over her and she was more than what her grandfather's abuse told her she was.

Every time he committed an act of abuse, he sent a message to Anna—a message that became clearer as the years passed. It was a message of disregard and disrespect, of deceit and brainwashing: "You're trash, and I can use you the way I want." This horrific luring of an innocent girl into his perversity set in motion a way of thinking that almost destroyed this young sweetheart.

The response to this kind of abuse is not what most would think. I learned years ago at a "Hope for the Wounded Heart" seminar by Dan Allender that girls can respond to sexual abuse by becoming party girls, bad girls, or good girls. Anna chose the good-girl route. She felt compelled to prove the message her grandfather communicated countless times through the years was wrong. She was going to make herself perfect. She set out to be valued, adored, and honored.

But Anna could not do this by herself. All her efforts could not quite fill the emptiness created by a selfish, uncontrolled man. As a result, she lived in a world of frustration and quiet rage, trying to erase the message she received for years. She just could not quite do it.

I have come to believe loss of any kind is one of the greatest motivators for behavior. It is why many teens do what they do. This cause-and-effect style of living is a response to damage done to us rather than a fulfillment of God's purpose in us. If we allow him, God can use loss for our benefit. He takes what was meant for evil and uses it for good. Loss impacts how we live, and teens are no exception.

What Is Loss?

When I talk about loss, I am talking about the voids in life that come from not getting what you want, need, or hope for. Loss is the chasm in the heart caused by deprivation, failure to achieve something, or possibly a defeat you experienced. It is the hollowness you are unable to overcome. It is a pit of loneliness that remains when something is taken away.

In times of loss, the gospel message is desperately needed. One of the greatest acts God performs for the person who experiences loss is to fill the voids and chasms created by that loss and give the true freedom that comes only in a relationship with Christ.

The hole in Anna's life because of sexual abuse cannot be filled by anything she does or does not do. It can only be filled by God. How does He do it? I have no idea, but I know He does. When Anna allows Him to do His work in her, she will no longer have to waste her time trying to fill voids. Instead, she will be able to fulfill her purpose in life, acknowledge His thumbprint on her life, and accept the role He calls her to fill.

After one of our seminars, a forty-year-old fellow told me, "All my life I have lived to overcome one comment made to me when I was in sixth grade." A teacher barked out a harsh remark that belittled and humiliated this man in front of the class. "If you had as much brains as you do fat, you might make something of yourself!" This teacher probably had no idea how much her one hurtful statement would negatively affect a little boy's life. So much so that he was still trying to get its echo out of his head almost thirty years later.

This man experienced a profound loss. A loss of value, respect, dignity, and honor. His thinking and behavior changed. He committed to prove that teacher wrong, to show everyone else he was not fat and he was smart. He lived from that day on with an "I'll-show-you" mentality. He was controlled by the lie of a careless, cruel teacher rather than by the One who created him and called Him "Son."

As you read these words, maybe something from your early years popped into your head. Perhaps your dad told you that you were stupid, or your mom said you were an embarrassment to the family. Maybe something remains buried deep in your soul, and the message still rings in your head when you are still. Most people experience some type of loss, especially today's young people. You may have learned to live with the lie, stuff it down, work to overcome it, or heal from it. Today's teens often do not know how to combat lies planted deep in their spirits. The wounds are open and bleeding, and their behavior shows their pain if you know how to look.

A father of one of the young men living with us at Heartlight shared how he spent most of his life trying to live down a comment his dad made during his teen years. His dad never told him he was proud of him and stated many times he did not think his son would amount to much. This man went on to share that he was now fifty years old and spent his adult life trying to please his father. Now he realized he should have been trying to please God.

When Scripture tells us about the fruit of the Spirit in Galatians 5:22-23, the last quality on the list is self-control. I submit to you this last fruit means more than anger management or squelching lust. I believe God calls us to exercise self-control so we are not controlled or even distracted by anything that could derail us from His intent and purpose for us.

Self-control means responding to what God has done for you, not reacting to what others have done to you.

This is an important concept to grasp as you attempt to understand your teen's behavior. We outlined how behavior is driven by needs. The question you need to ask now is the following: Has a loss in my child's life caused a need that his or her behavior is trying to fill?

Scripture tells us God is the spring of living water. You can drink all the water you want, but until you drink from Him, you will always thirst. My efforts to satisfy my needs will only temporarily satisfy my thirst. His provision fully meets my need, ending my thirst and eliminating the need for me to find my own refreshment.

Jeremiah 2:13 (NIV) states it beautifully: "My people have committed two sins: They have forsaken me, the spring of living water, and have dug their own cisterns, broken cisterns that cannot hold water."

When we listen to the negative comments and criticisms of others and allow the lies to take root in our spirits, we are like broken cisterns. We continue to thirst and pour in addictive behaviors, sexual promiscuity, inappropriate relationships—anything we can to try to keep the leaking cistern full. Only when we hear the voice of truth and allow His living water to remove the lies will our cisterns be whole.

Moods of a Lifetime

Jan and I had the honor of living at a Christian sports camp in Branson, Mo., named Kanakuk Kamp. We lived there for seven years back in the 1980s. We had an incredibly wonderful time of learning as we rubbed shoulders with people from around the country and from all walks of life.

One of the joys of our time there was getting to know Spike and Darnell White. While both have since passed, the impact they had on Jan and me will never be forgotten. Spike was an eighty-something man who made everyone around him feel valuable, especially me. I had numerous opportunities to dive into deep discussions with Spike about why kids do what they do, what gets them off track, and how to work with kids who were struggling. I will never forget a statement he made that appeared on much of the camp's literature: "The moods of a lifetime are often set in the all-but-forgotten events of child-hood."

Spike wanted people to provide great opportunities for kids that would help mold their character, destiny, and purpose in life. His statement remains undoubtedly true. Childhood events have the power to positively or negatively affect a person's life for decades.

Jamie

Jamie is a young lady from Virginia who was shy, distrustful of people, self-centered, and protective in her conversations. She wanted to engage in deep, personal discussions; but she just could not because she did not trust anyone.

One day I asked her parents about her past. I asked a barrage of questions about her family, her social interactions, and her medical history. Jamie's parents adopted her from Social Services in Richmond, Va., when she was one-and-a-half years old. They knew the time Jamie spent with her birth parents was rough, but they assured me they did not think that was the cause of her behavior now. It couldn't be, could it? Jamie was too little then to remember that time. Right?

Jamie's parents then described how traumatic her first eighteen months were. By the time this girl was three, she had to undergo surgery to repair rips and tears in her vagina because of sexual abuse from her birth father. When she was a toddler, her birth father intentionally broke her arm because she made a mess at dinner. Jamie's parents shared stories of neglect and abuse, medical conditions, and suffering before Social Services intervened in the situation. Again, they assured me Jamie had no memory of any of the incidents.

While they were telling me this, my granddaughter Maile, who was a year-and-a-half at the time, ran around our Heartlight conference center. I looked at her, imagining the damage if anyone did the same to her. I looked at the parents and asked, "Do you really think all of those terrible events never affected Jamie because she can't remember anything?" I then asked them, "What if I asked Maile to come over to me, grabbed her arm, and broke it? Do you think she would not remember it five years from now? That it would not affect her?" They were silent, and I thought, *Good night, you've got to be kidding me!*

Jamie experienced great losses in her life. The loss of trust, innocence, safety, and protection, to name just a few, caused a mind-set that led to her behaviors now as a teen. Her subconscious remembered it. Of course, it affected her! The moods of a lifetime can be set by the all-but-forgotten and the forgotten (but still in the subconscious) good and bad events in one's life.

Understanding Your Child's Loss

Every time I mention losses in a presentation, some parents ask, "What if we can't pinpoint any losses?" Good question.

I usually ask if they had losses during their early years. Most say "yes." Then I ask, "Did your parents know about them?" Most say "no." I then ask, "Could you perhaps not know everything that has happened to your child?"

The losses may not appear to be significant or remarkable. Remember when your child used to come to you and tell you, "Sally said I was stupid," and you countered it to reassure your child?

"You're not stupid," you probably said. "Don't listen to Sally; she doesn't know you." Or you might have responded, "Sweetheart, that's not true. You're one of the smartest people I know." Now jump ahead a few years to junior high. Does a middle school child still tell you about the comments from other kids? Probably not.

Why? Because kids begin to believe some of those comments. They will not come to us, so we must go to them.

We must enter their world, ask what's going on in their lives, and uncover the hurt and pain they are experiencing.

Another situation where kids experience loss is divorce and remarriage. Many stepparents do not understand why they are not accepted by the new stepchildren. Often, I find it is because the stepparent represents loss. A stepparent means the dream of parents getting back together is gone. It means the loss of bounding into the single parent's bedroom and plopping down on the bed. (Now there is a stranger in there!) Sometimes it means a child loses a house, a school, and friends if the stepfamily moves. The new stepmother gets frustrated as she tries as hard as she can to connect with the new kids. She cannot bridge the chasm because she reminds her stepkids of loss.

What is a parent or stepparent to do? Deal with the loss. In fact, dealing with the loss is more important than trying to change the behavior. Focus on the cause rather than the symptoms. David Damico, in his book *The Faces of Rage*, states, "Often repressed or forgotten, such childhood losses tend to re-emerge at significant transition points of change in the adult's life. This shows that unresolved loss is never resolved merely through the passage of time."[1]

Focus on dealing with the loss, whether it is a loss of self-esteem from hurtful comments, the loss of the traditional family, the loss of innocence taken, or any other kind of loss that comes into a child's life. This is much easier when losses are pretty visible, such as the death of a parent, the loss of a loved one, a breakup, or the death of a friend. It is a little harder when the loss is hidden under the surface. Whether apparent or not, if your children are acting out, look hard for any loss they are trying to deal with.

What Does Loss Look Like?

For many young people, loss can be an unmet expectation. They believe things should be different than they are. They think people don't understand them, listen to them, or pay attention to them. They think life should be fair and just, and they discover it is not.

When children feel this way, they try to eliminate the loss or cover it up. The development of strong, healthy relationships is going to be the key to help them through these tough times.

More often than not, the relationship should be with a parent or other adult, not a peer.

Losses in kids' lives may also come as a result of the actions of others. When children experience this kind of loss, they pay the price for the foolish choices and behaviors of other people. These losses include car accidents, others' mistakes, or situations where kids are the victims of others' bad judgments.

Loss can also come from abuse or neglect by parents or caregivers. When parents do not provide what a child needs, or when parents break the law and are caught, kids pay a price for the parents' selfish behavior. Loss may come from societal prejudice, which has nothing to do with the children and more to do with those who display their shortcomings with damaging words and actions.

Why is it important to know the various types of loss a child may experience? Each type of loss creates its own set of questions and issues. When kids are victims of others' bad choices, they ask questions—not about other people or about themselves, but about life and about God:

Why do bad things happen to good people?

If God is such a loving God, why did He allow this to happen?

If life is good, why do I always feel so bad?

Why do I feel as if God doesn't like me?

Is this part of God's will for my life?

Why has God ignored me?

Is life just a crapshoot?

Throughout my life I have heard the phrase, "If God is for us, who can be against us?" But what if you are a young person who says, "No one is for me, and God is against me?" Kids need special help working through this kind of loss. They need spiritual discussions that can bring light into their darkness.

Another type of loss comes from dashed hopes, unfulfilled dreams, or postponed pursuits. This kind of loss includes not reaching a goal or taking advantage of an opportunity. It is not making the team, not getting the cheerleading spot, not being good enough to qualify for something desperately desired. This type of loss is focused inward and usually includes shame, guilt, and emptiness. When a young person believed in and hoped for something, then realizes it is not going to happen, reality is a bitter pill to swallow.

When a child realizes how things really are, parents might see a shutdown or a sudden shift in their child's interests. If this happens with your child, do not add to your child's burden with a discouraging comment like, "I told you so," or, "Well, you should have listened to me." Come alongside your child with heartfelt statements like, "I know this is hard." Do not make it any less than it feels to your child, and help your child not to make it any more than it is.

Finally, some losses result from changes to a child's life that are out of his or her control, such as a cross-country move or a natural disaster. Avoid saying, "Well, that's just the way it is." Rather, be sensitive to your child and work hard at listening and hearing your child's heart. In these situations, your child will often feel like life is not fair, and no one can do anything about it. This is the category of loss an adopted child may experience. The adoptee had no control over the loss of biological parents or the placement in an adoptive family.

By the way, a young person told me once: "Adoption is the only trauma where we are expected to be thankful." Debate that all you want, but this young person is expressing a loss. She was not discounting what she gained, just acknowledging her loss. All of us would do well to recognize the difference between the two. Medical conditions, changes in personal appearance, and inherited afflictions can also create this kind of loss.

When Does Loss Happen?

It happens when a child realizes it. I never knew I had skinny legs until someone called me "Chicken Legs." I never knew my nose was big until a comment was made during seventh grade. I hardly knew I spent years not being able to read a blackboard until I put on a pair of glasses when I was fourteen. I never thought I had any losses from my dad until I had my own son and began to wonder why my dad never spent any time with me. Jan never realized her normal really was not normal until someone told her she should tell her mom.

Brendan

Brendan lost his dad in the World Trade Center disaster on September 11, 2001. He was so young at the time he still thought in concrete terms. He realized his dad was gone, adjustments had to be made, and concrete (and understandable) needs had to be met around the home. He was now the "man" of the household. More chores had to be done, the dog needed a new caretaker, and Mommy would take over some of Dad's jobs.

When Brendan turned fourteen, his thinking shifted from concrete to abstract. He slowly realized Dad would never see him play basketball, would not be there when he got his driver's license, and would not attend his high school graduation or drop him off at college. His dad would not be at his wedding or someday hold his children. As Brendan's new awareness blossomed, so did inappropriate ways of handling the pain he began feeling. His behavior eventually landed him at Heartlight.

Where was the loss? It happened on 9/11. It continued to play out as Brendan grew up without a dad. It happened all over again when adolescence caused Brendan to look at the tragedy with the new understanding of a maturing abstract intellect. His behaviors tried to fill the new voids he felt in his life. They would not change until mentors helped Brendan recognize, face, and deal with the losses he experienced.

Response to Loss

A loss-free childhood is not an indicator of good parenting, nor is a loss-riddled childhood necessarily a sign of terrible parenting. The bumper sticker that says, "Stuff happens" could just as easily say, "Loss happens." It is inevitable at some point that human beings will experience loss. Wise parents understand their own losses and how those losses affected (or still affect) them. Then they are able to more easily recognize loss in their children's lives and move toward them to help in difficult times.

Most kids try to tell you losses are not that big of a deal. They minimize them, hoping to minimize the pain. I have to break the news of a family member's death to kids sometimes and see them respond, "Well, I really didn't know her that well anyway," or "It's no big deal," or "I am okay. I am fine." Don't believe it.

I encourage you to give your children the freedom to respond to the hurt of any loss. They need to let off some emotional steam. That does not mean you allow a cavalcade of emotions to control your children and destroy your home. Just give your children permission to become undone once in a while. As they express their pain, move toward them relationally.

When will children see their losses? Who knows? Maybe not for years. A young girl may realize her loss when she sees all the other girls with their dads and realizes she does not have one to hang out with her. A boy who tried out for the basketball team may feel the loss of being cut as he sits in the stands and watches the team practice for a game.

If you did not experience a close relationship with one or both of your parents, you may feel a sense of loss if you have a great relationship with your son or daughter. Or if your parents are better grandparents than they were parents. The good times you have with your child may cause you to grieve what could have been with your own folks.

I feel the loss of four kids who were dear to me whenever I hear the names Caroline, Todd, Cindy, or Darren. My wife remembers her loss whenever she smells Old Spice aftershave. Memories of losses can pop up anytime, anyplace. They can be triggered by anything. Some of the behavior we see from young people can be their way of avoiding or filling the void created by those losses.

Impact of Loss

Understanding loss does not give you all the answers to inappropriate and potentially dangerous behavior. But it does provide an opportunity to try a different approach toward your children, even if they don't understand their loss. As we have seen, your child's behavior is not really the issue. It is just an indicator of the struggle that lies beneath the surface.

As you gently probe your child's losses, you may stir the pain of your own losses. Your response to loss may create some behavior patterns in you that cause some negative reactions from your spouse or kids. It's never too late to look at the log in your own eye.

Introspection and reflection are acts of wisdom.

In fact, I believe in order to deal with a child's loss, parents need to understand the impact of loss in their own lives. I suggest you find someone to talk with about your life. Consider a counselor or a concerned pastor. Look for a women or men's group where people talk about their experiences and feelings. Keep looking until you find someone you can talk to about the things in your past that need some attention.

Loss is big in all our lives. If you spend time searching and understanding the damage in your life, you might discover why certain people respond negatively to you in certain situations. You may begin to understand what your child is going through.

Perhaps the damage in your life is getting in the way of your relationship with your child. Maybe you transfer the damage in your life to your child. If either of these is true, you can take steps to heal.

My losses impacted my thinking, behavior, and expectations. However, I did not know it until someone showed me the truth. I avoided facing the damage done to me in my life. Without other people's help, I would never have seen it or known it existed, let alone faced it and healed from it.

People respond to losses in various ways, but the place to start connecting is always the same. You start where they hurt. For instance, the teens who live with us at Heartlight probably cannot tell you about their losses, but they can tell you where they hurt. We start by helping these kids through their pain in a setting where we can control their behavior. That environment gives them a chance to reflect on the damage done to them. As a result, they realize how loss plays a big part in their lives.

Most kids who experience loss feel like damaged goods.

They may spend the rest of their lives trying to feel whole again. Their self-value is diminished. They use selfishness to try to compensate for their loss. They do not know what a healthy life looks like, and this makes them angry and confused. They begin to behave in ways that bring false and temporary value.

These kids begin the process of a slow death because they are driven by self-centered motives to preserve what they have and regain what they lost. Avoidance becomes a priority, and a facade of confidence cloaks pain and hurt.

These are tough days for teens. But they are also the best days to offer a message, a relationship, some wisdom, and perhaps a taste of something beyond themselves. Something that might touch their hearts so they catch a glimpse of a greater One who loves them more than they could ever imagine.

Losses can keep us from what God intends for us, prevent us from fulfilling our real purpose, and hinder our movement toward becoming the people God desires us to be. Dealing with loss can consume us and take so much of our time we never become what we were intended to be. Or loss can move us toward Him, toward our healing, toward light, and toward our true value and purpose. This happens best when someone guides us out of the darkness. That is what you can do for your child.

Ephesians 2:10 (NIV) states, "For we are God's handiwork, created in Christ Jesus to do good works, which God prepared in advance for us to do." God has a plan and direction for each of our lives, and losses can cause a detour. They can move us away from His intent, His preparation, and His purpose. No wonder people are so frustrated in life and teens are so mad.

My wife was not created for her grandfather's abuse or enjoyment. Jamie was not created to suffer her father's abuse. Young men are not supposed to grow up wondering whether they have more fat than brains. We were not made for any of this.

That is why it is so important to understand the loss(es) your child might be experiencing and to use that understanding to change your child's mind-set and behavior. Otherwise, your child will carry the baggage of life's losses well into his adulthood. Pain and hardship may plague her for a lifetime. Or you can seek healing for your losses and your children's, understand the real reasons for their behavior, and forge a bond of love and empathy. That kind of effort can break the chains of loss and create a healthy environment in which both of you walk in joy, fulfilling your passions and purpose and serving the God who loves you.

"I will give thanks to You, for I am fearfully and
wonderfully made;
Wonderful are Your works,
And my soul knows it very well" (Psalm 139:14 NASB).

CHAPTER NINE

PUTTING YOUR KNOWLEDGE TO WORK

*W*ould you love a quick fix for all the problems you have with the kids in your home? Would you like to wake up one morning and find everything is different? Do you wish all the changes you would like to see in your family could happen at the snap of your fingers?

Sure you would. Who wouldn't? Quick fixes sound great. Unfortunately, they don't work.

Getting Your House in Order

As I mentioned very early in this book, chances are you are reading these pages because something is not right. Or maybe you think something might go wrong in your teen's life, and you are preparing yourself.

The first step is to get your house in order. It can still be relaxed, operating as planned chaos, but it must be in order. Getting your house in order must be strategic, deliberate, and calculated because the process of change takes time. I have seen again and again that when parents develop a plan, most homes quickly begin moving toward health. Let me offer an effective, six-step approach to making changes in your home:

1. Identify the Things That Must Change

Let me ask you a question: If your children continue to do the same things they are doing now, where will your child be in six months? Where will your family be in five years? If you do not like the answers, then something must change between now and then. Today is a great day to get started. What would you like to see changed? What would you like to be different?

Ask yourself the question, "What bothers me the most about what is happening in my family?" Then start looking at changes that need to happen in the areas of your home that need improvement.

Sit down with a pad of paper and write down what you like in your home and what you don't like. While doing this exercise, do not let the problems you caused get in the way of the changes you want to see. You are not a perfect parent, but your position of authority means you can still require changes. You are not bound by what you did or did not do years earlier or by mistakes you made in the past that you cannot reverse. You are older and wiser now. It's time to move on.

Forgiveness means you stop hoping for a better past. Instead, plan a better future.

List the things that are wrong. Be real and honest with yourself. Change cannot begin until we accept that problems exist.

2. Set the Stage for Change

The second step to a more stable family is to set the stage for change. Sit down with your children and share with them that your family needs to make some changes. Even if you do not know what those changes should be, just say, "I am not sure what needs to change, but something needs to change."

Allow your kids to have input. Ask them what they would like to see changed in your family or your home. Whatever they say, listen first. Respond later. Wait until they say, "Well, Mom (or Dad), what would you like to see changed in our home or in our family?" Do not have a ready response. Tell them, "Good question. Let me think about it." If you answer, you take away the opportunity for your kids to reason for themselves about what needs to change and their role and responsibility in changing it.

Implementing your kids' suggestions is usually far better than implementing your own. You might say, "You know, guys, you are no longer little kids, and I think we still treat you like kids too much." Leave it at that. Again, listen for their responses. The conversation might go something like this:

"Come on, Dad. What do you mean?"

"I don't know. I just think we should not treat you like little kids anymore."

See what's happening? You are setting the stage for change.

You can tell them, "Mom can not continue to do this anymore," or, "I know things have been kind of strained, and I want things to be different," or, "Guys, we have a problem, and something's gotta give," or just a statement that says, "I think I am losing you, and I can't stand back and do nothing." This one is tough because a child may protest or ask "What do you mean?" Do not answer. Just say, "I don't know. I just feel like I am losing you." You are helping them think, preparing them for change, and enlisting their assistance so everyone can recognize and work through the problems together.

3. Prepare Your Family for Change

After you spend time setting the stage (perhaps a few days later), begin to communicate the problems you see in your home and family. Do not dump everything at once. Start with a couple of things.

Perhaps the main issue in your home is disrespect. You could say, "Son, let's get together and discuss what I mentioned last week." If he does not want to get together, encourage him in some way, saying, "Hey, let's go get something to eat" (at his favorite restaurant). If worse comes to worse and your son refuses to meet, take something away that is important to him, such as the car, cell phone, Internet access, PlayStation, Xbox, or whatever it takes to get his attention. He may yell, "That's not fair. You're manipulating me!"

You can say, "I know, but that is how important it is for us to talk. When do you want to get together?" Then suggest a time. The lesson here is to ask and invite first, then demand. It's an old horse-training rule that also works well with teens.

If he is still not ready, do not ask anymore. If he continues to balk, take more away. Let him feel pain until conversation occurs.

Relationship is more important than your child's possessions, friends, or activities.

You may have to force his hand.

This may be a new stance for you, particularly if you're a single parent. Single parenting is tough. It is born of loss. That shared loss moves parent and child together. An easy way to survive is for the parent and the kids to become peers. However, the single parent will face a hard time moving back into the parent role—the role of the authority—if he or she always acts like a friend. This becomes especially tough if the parent remarries. It is a necessary and important move to regain your proper parental role in order to confront issues in your home.

4. Reevaluate Your Role with Your Child

It's hard to change your role with your child. If you act as a peer or friend, "breaking up" with that role is critical to your child's healthy progress and to establish a healthy home in the teen years. If you are easygoing, a nondisciplinarian, it will feel uncomfortable to you and frustrating to your child when you try to establish and exert authority you never exercised in the past.

Single moms and dads have to fulfill both parental roles. Sometimes it is tough to switch back and forth in order to provide what both parents usually provide.

A mom instills value. A dad validates it.

A mom pushes for relationship. A dad pushes for maturity.

A mom nurtures. A dad confronts.

My point is not so much about who-does-what. I use these descriptions to help you understand there are different roles parents fulfill. When the needs of your kids change, the roles you play need to change as well.

The one who focused primarily on relationship through the years might now exert more authority in order to confront inappropriate behavior. Your teen gets to see you in a whole new light. She may not like it. Expect conflict. You can both handle it. You will both get through it. Stand strong, Mom or Dad. Now is the time your teen needs your wisdom and guidance the most, whether she wants it or not.

You may want to talk to your teen about your changing role with any of the following openers:

"Hey, I need to put on the 'Mom hat' here and share some things with you."

"Sweetheart, I told you I would always be honest with you. I need to tell you some things that are hard for me to say."

"Son, you and I have always had a great relationship. I do not want to do anything to damage that, but we need to talk about some stuff before our relationship is ruined."

"This is hard for me to say, but I think some things need to be said."

"I have never played the 'Dad role' before, but I need to now."

"I am not perfect, but I do have some ideas about how we can get better as a family."

"I am not good at confronting things, and it seems like you always talk your way out of anything I say. However, there are some things we need to talk about. Will you listen and let me speak, so I can share what's on my heart?"

5. Communicate the Change

The next step in moving towards healthy changes within your family is to communicate the change. This is the beginning stage of implementing your new changes and direction. Start by communicating what you want to see changed. You can say, "Here are the changes, and this is what we would like to do differently." You may have allowed some attitudes or actions in your family that are now no longer acceptable. Now is your opportunity to say, "We were wrong, and we are going to change direction so our family can be healthy and our relationships loving and strong."

6. Implement the Plan for Change

The sixth step is where you begin to see the change. Often, this will be more painful than you expect. It will bring conflict. To the point you will be tempted to back down and let the *status quo* remain in your home. Don't give in now!

This is your chance to use what you learned from the first chapters of this book. You know when to be strong and when to be sensitive. You know your kids need to be allowed to go through some temporary pain in order to learn the consequences of inappropriate behavior. This is when parents—whether together, separated, or divorced—should implement the plan in one accord.

This is also the crucial time when your children try to figure out how serious you are about change. They will push buttons, test limits, go outside the boundaries, and assess your genuineness and dedication to the process of getting your house in order. They will learn whether you are capable of following through on what you said and whether you truly believe in what you are doing.

This is where rules and consequences kick in and must be consistent. Determining the rules and consequences for your family is one of the best ways to communicate what you would like your home to look like. (I will unpack this more with practical suggestions in a later chapter.)

Do these six steps sound easy? Maybe. Maybe not. Will they be easy? Definitely not. Breaking a horse sounds easy. The actual process is grueling, as anyone who works with horses can testify. Rarely do family members all agree in the initial stages of implementing new ideas that will cause pain, frustration, or a loss of power, control or freedom. However, on the other side of these temporary discomforts you will find deeper relationships, healthier people, and more stability as a family.

The Foolish, the Wise, and the Repentant

We are foolish if we believe we must achieve happiness on our own terms without consideration of God or dependence on Him, our families, or anyone else. We are foolish when we are so convinced we are right we will not listen when others try to help. Foolish people believe they can handle it all if everyone just leaves them alone.

Foolishness is self-centeredness at its apex and selfishness in all its glory.

Foolishness leads to more and more pain. Unless someone else gets involved, a foolish person usually will not turn around and come to his senses until he is eating out of a garbage can in some back alley. (Anyone remember a guy called the Prodigal Son?)

Scripture tells us "Foolishness is bound up in the heart of a child; The rod of discipline will remove it far from him" (Proverbs 22:15 NASB). Of course, this does not mean you beat a child into changing. Your "rod of discipline" might be the car keys. It might be grounding. It might be other consequences or privileges taken away.

People tell me all the time young people "need their clock cleaned a couple of times and they'd straighten up." I agree adolescents and teens need to feel pain and discomfort from wrong actions and behavior, but pain comes in more forms than corporal or physical punishment.

Then they say, "Well, it worked for me. It should work for them. I mean, you train horses the same way you did a hundred years ago, don't ya?"

My answer? No. Plus, children are not horses. The world is completely different than it was twenty years ago. The culture has changed. Kids' opportunities have changed. Their possessions have changed. Their amount of exposure to immorality, addictions, nontraditional families and lifestyles has changed. Their styles, likes and dislikes, and interactions have changed.

We did not have social media, Internet, or cell phones when we were young. Kids today have access not only to their peers twenty-four hours a day, seven days a week, but also to total strangers! Getting whacked with a leather belt does not work anymore. Plus, in this culture, it could get you arrested. You can not help your kid change his behavior if you are stuck behind bars.

The issue at hand, and the encouragement of Scripture, is not to take a literal rod to your children. Rather, you need to use an effective form of discipline to get your children to stop what they are doing anytime their actions will damage their lives and relationships if they continue.

Use whatever type of discipline will be effective with your kids. Just have the courage to use something. Any rod of discipline that creates pain and discomfort in the lives of your children will move them in a new direction. When they move to something else, pray and coach them to make a wiser choice than the ones they chose before. Where do they get input for that next choice?

From you, Mom.

From you, Dad.

In contrast to foolishness, wisdom is the application of the principles of right living. It is gained through observation, reflection, and experience. What your children watch, what they think about, and what they do give them opportunities to gain wisdom to make better choices and healthier decisions.

Kids probably will not like it you when you begin to get your house in order. However, later they will love you for your right stance and willingness to face conflict and stand firm in order to achieve something better.

The momentary pain that creates change is a small price to pay for the greater reward of helping a child mature and gain wisdom by stopping childish behavior.

Use temporary discomfort to move your child to repentance and change. By the way, I define repentance as the recognition of false images and beliefs related to meeting personal needs, and the forsaking of those images and beliefs for a commitment to and dependence on God, your family, and others. In other words, true repentance means you are not only sorry for what you did, but also willing to make amends and move in a different direction from that moment forward.

Most parents want change within their family but do not know how to get it. Or they want change but do nothing because they are afraid of their children's responses. As a result, the children control the home, determine the atmosphere, and thwart any attempt to restore order. Parents become numb to their children's behavior and retreat from relationship, which only allows their children to continue on the path to destruction. Parents may not even realize the level of depravity their children have moved toward. They silently watch their children deteriorate, the whole family dying inside from the pain.

Helping Teens Gain Wisdom

Here come some questions that might sting a little. What does your teen observe from watching you? When your adolescent finishes a discussion with you, is she glad it is over? Or does he leave challenged and wanting to know more? What is your child's favorite memory with you? Do you know how to help your kids gain wisdom?

Let me expound on each of these a bit to make sure you understand what I am trying to say. Have you heard these old sayings?

Actions speak louder than words

It's not what you say, it's what you do.

Don't talk, just act. Don't say, just show. Don't promise, just prove.

I don't trust words. I trust actions.

Applying these to the Christian life means the gospel is more "caught" than "taught." I remember a fellow telling me once he could not hear what I was saying because my actions were speaking too loudly. Now I am asking you: Do your actions support your words? Do you live the way you tell your teen to live? Do your kids hear one thing but see another?

Especially in the adolescent and teen years, your children watch you closely. When your kids were little, they looked up to you, idolized you, basically worshipped the ground you walked on. Once puberty hits and thinking changes, parents topple right off the pedestal. Suddenly, your child sees your flaws—all of them. He may even think he sees some that aren't there. You went from brilliant to idiotic seemingly overnight, all because some dreaded hormones reared their ugly heads in your child's body and brain.

It is not fun, but it is totally normal. What you need to remember is that from now on, how you "walk" will be far more important than the way you talk.

Be careful what you say. Be even more careful what you display.

Between the time your children's heads hit their pillows and their eyes finally call it quits each day, what do they think about? Are they mulling over the conversations you had that day or cussing you out, trying to get you and your anger or hypocrisy out of their minds?

I always try to leave kids with a question, something to get them to think and reflect on the words I share. I hope they will take the information and counsel I offer and apply it to their lives and their culture.

Are the experiences you have with your teen mere entertainment or interactions that make memories for a lifetime? I encourage you to create experiences with your child during their teen years that accomplish two things: the first is to provide life lessons they retain and apply, and the second is to give the life lesson within the context of an activity that will build your relationship. What does that look like?

Here are three stories of parents who decided to get their houses in order and exercise some discipline. These parents determined to stop their children's destructive behavior and help them discover what they were doing was unacceptable.

Angel

Sixteen-year-old Angel chose to simply ignore her mom and dad. Even when they tried to create an opportunity for discussion or confronted her, Angel belittled and demeaned. She verbally attacked her parents, then withdrew. She used a litany of abuse to shut down everything Mom or Dad would say.

"Deal with it, Dad."

"Shut up, Mom. You can't tell me what to do."

"You guys are so wrong. Who do you think you are?"

"Screw you, Dad! I am leaving."

"Why do you always point the finger at me when you're just as screwed up?"

"Why don't you look in the mirror?"

"Get over it. Nobody's perfect."

"I can't wait until I can leave this house!"

Whenever Mom or Dad tried to talk to Angel, she glared at one of them, rolled her eyes, and walked away in disgust. She then acted as if her parents were not even in the room. Her most famous act was to put in the earbuds from her iPod and turn up the music whenever Mom started talking to her, thus drowning Mom out. Not exactly behavior that would win her the Miss Congeniality Award.

When I first met Angel and watched her unleash one of her volleys of verbal trash on her parents, I wondered, *How did this young lady ever get the name Angel?* (I have to admit I also thought I could come up with a more appropriate name.) I chuckled inside, watching this girl try to act above us all. In fact, she reduced herself to something lower than most kids I see. And that's saying something, because in the past forty years I have seen a lot.

For some reason, Angel's style of relating to her parents was working for her. Her foolishness was extreme. She was loud, rude, and mean. It did not seem to bother her a bit. If someone did not stop Angel, she was headed to a sorry place in her relationships. No wonder this young lady had no friends and could not keep a job. She was so offensive she pushed people away.

After meeting with Angel's parents, I asked if they were ready for things to get worse. Placing restrictions around Angel would probably result in more intense attacks. They were scared to death. These poor parents knew they had to do something, but they were so fearful of her response their pattern was to freeze up and walk away.

I met with them a few times to help them put together some rules and consequences for their home, focusing on only a few immediate things that needed to change. Our goal was to keep Angel from moving out. I offered these instructions for determining the rules for their home:

1. Write down five things you would like to see changed in Angel's behavior.

2. Put those things in a letter and give it to her. (Discussion was not getting anywhere.)

3. In the letter, set a time to spend thirty minutes to talk about it. Let her know Mom or Dad will do all the talking.

4. Whatever her response, drop it. This is not the time to prove you are serious. That comes later. Keep the conversation geared around statements like, "No more," and, "This is where we stand."

5. Communicate the new rules clearly.

Here is their set of new rules for Angel:

1. Angel must immediately stop disrespectfully ignoring Mom and Dad.

2. Angel must immediately stop her cutting comments and accusations.

3. Even if Angel rejects Mom and Dad, they will never reject her.

4. Dad (or Mom) will eat breakfast with Angel once a week at a restaurant of her choice.

5. Angel will not belittle or display arrogance or meanness toward anyone in the family. (The school would need to deal with issues at school, and her friends would have to deal with her on their level.)

6. Any violation or disregard of the first five rules will result in consequences, including loss of the car, no car insurance, and no cell phone. In addition, Angel may have to ride the bus to school (or walk), she might not receive money for clothes, and she could lose the computer and the iPod.

Angel's Dad handed her the letter, and her first comment was, "What's this?" Dad told her it was a letter outlining some things they would like to see different in their home. She tore it in half, threw it down, and stormed out of the house. Dad called me, and I told him to put the torn letter on her pillow for her to read later that night. He did.

Angel came home, read the letter, and stormed into her parents' room. She could not ignore this. Her volley began, and they listened quietly. When Angel finished, her dad simply said, "It starts tomorrow." (I think he must have been given divine inspiration right then, not to mention a saint's patience.)

Angel was pretty calm the next few days. When I talked with her parents, I told them, "That's what they said about Mount St. Helens a few days before the volcano's explosion. Just wait."

After three days, Angel's old ugliness returned. Now Mom and Dad had to follow through. They did, and Angel's response was the same as before. This time, however, she reacted in disbelief that Mom and Dad were actually going to do something. They held firm.

A word to the wise: Like training horses, once you start disciplining your child, you ca not stop or the behavior will only get worse. Angel's comments and disrespectful behavior continued, and her parents took away more and more privileges over the next three months. Angel finally got the picture. The weekly breakfasts were pretty quiet for a while. Eventually, Angel wanted to talk rather than sit in the uncomfortable silence. Because her parents were consistent with the consequences over the previous months, Angel finally began to engage rather than belittle.

The three months of pain were beginning to pay off for everyone. A new day was dawning with the beginnings of real relationship between Angel and her parents. Angel and I even laugh together at the way she acted during all the conflict. I called her DD for "Devil in Disguise." It's a nickname I still jokingly remind her of whenever we talk.

Charlie

Seventeen-year-old Charlie lived like a hermit. He buried his head in the sand of his room. He disconnected, disengaged, and disassociated from everyone and everything. Something shut him down, and his mom could not figure out what it was. She and I talked about his poor school performance, missed classes, and whether this smart young man could get into college someday.

When I finally met with Charlie (which he agreed to only because his mother threatened to take away the DVD player in his room), he seemed like a pretty cool young man. Still, something was stirring below the surface. He would not talk about it.

He was not aggressive—actively or passively. Nor was he verbally abusive. This sounded more alarms for me than more intense behavior would have. I feared Charlie was despondent and despairing. I was not concerned about what Charlie might be doing; I was concerned that he was doing nothing. Usually, kids want something. Charlie didn't. Most teens are motivated toward something, but Charlie was not.

The only things Charlie cared about were his guitar, his music, his computer games, and his cat, Dork. At this point, school, friends, activities, privileges, and possessions meant nothing. He just existed alone in his room. He would not eat meals with his sister and mother. He would not get out of bed until noon. He just did not care. If anyone tried to talk to him about where he was headed in life, he started crying and quit talking.

Oddly, Charlie and his mom had a good relationship. However, she protected him, enabling him to live in his own world. Charlie was not going to change unless someone forced that change. Mom needed to be that catalyst. My counsel to Charlie's mom was pretty simple:

1. Take the blinds off the bedroom windows.

2. Tell Charlie he is going to a counselor if he wants Internet access in the home. (I told her to turn it off any week he doesn't go.)

3. Explain to Charlie if he wants to flunk out of school he can, but then he cannot be home during the day when she is not there. (This meant she would probably have to change the locks.)

4. Inform Charlie if he does not go to school but wants to live at home, he has to get a job.

5. Let him know meals are to be eaten in the kitchen with everyone else.

Pretty simple advice, right? But these five steps were not the end of the process. Taking the blinds off the bedroom windows was a tactic to show change was coming, and it allowed the sun to start the waking process each morning. Charlie went to the counselor, who recommended medication. It was Charlie's responsibility to take it if he wanted to continue to live at home.

Getting Charlie out of the house during the day rocked his world and changed his environment. Even hanging out at Starbucks brought interaction with other people and gave the counselor some easy topics to discuss. Charlie got a job, and it taught him the value of people even more than it did the value of money. Making him eat meals at the table with everyone else forged some connection and eliminated his reclusive existence.

Notice how we chose each of the requirements to produce actions we hoped would move Charlie to a different place. The difficulty was getting Mom to quit enabling this young man. Changing her ways was painful for her. It forced her to try new approaches to get her house in order. The discomfort she endured probably saved her son's life. All it took was a little encouragement and clear understanding of what she wanted for and from her son.

Tracy

Tracy yelled, screamed, and cussed like a sailor when her parents tried to correct or discipline her. This fifteen-year-old's style was not to ignore or shut down. If it was fight or flight, she picked fight every time to get her way. She attacked with a vengeance.

She developed this response in order to avoid receiving input. Her tantrums shut everyone else down. They were much like a six-year-old's and absolutely inappropriate for any teen. If Mom or Dad tried to correct her while they were on vacation, out to dinner, or at church, Tracy got ugly real fast. Needless to say, her parents tried to avoid anything that would set Tracy off. Eventually, they avoided her in every way. They feared being put in an embarrassing situation. Everyone walked on eggshells around this girl and her temper.

Tracy's parents did not have to ask what the problem was. It was always in their face. Both parents started working more, spending more time together, working out more, and keeping busier at church, probably to stay away their daughter. This only fueled Tracy's anger and verbal abuse.

Tracy's behavior was pure poison, and she was one of the most demanding, self-centered, self-absorbed, arrogant, pathetic young ladies I ever met. Still, there was something special about her. She was kind to animals and loved little children. When she was not yelling and screaming, she could be very thoughtful. I knew something was triggering her behavior. To stand up to this young lady would be too much of a challenge for most people. When her parents looked to me for help, I applauded them for their patience and willingness to start doing battle.

My counsel to them combined consequences and incentives. I advised her parents to do the following:

1. Find out Tracy's favorite activities and possessions. This would help determine the rewards and consequences for her behavior.

2. Tell Tracy she would suffer penalties for any behavior that was not age-appropriate.

3. Let her know she would also be rewarded for meeting their standards for thirty days.

4. Choose a reward that was something she really wanted.

Tracy's bad behavior had become habit. Outbursts were a coping skill she acquired, unchallenged by Mom and Dad. Her bad temper worked for her until now. Because her parents allowed it for so long, it was fully ingrained in her personality.

I encouraged the family to hold to what was right and prepare themselves for a long haul of battles, confrontations, consequences, and turmoil. It was tough and it took a while, but Tracy eventually learned she needed to change. That process included stopping bad behaviors and learning new, better behavior.

Tracy's progress came slowly. In fact, her parents did not see any progress at all for more than a year. It took this young woman a year-and-a-half to win her first reward. Eventually, her parents' consistency in applying consequences and sticking to their family rules broke Tracy of the patterns that would have destroyed her relationships if her parents allowed them to continue.

What Is Normal Behavior Anymore?

Parents say all the time they don't know what normal is anymore. Here are some behaviors I think are pretty normal for teens today.

But remember, even if they are normal, some are unacceptable.

- Not wanting to do chores—and wanting everyone else to do things for them.

- Enjoying doing those same chores for other people.

- Putting off chores and then wanting to be paid for doing them.

- Showing anger when they don't get what they want.

- Forgetting to mow the yard and then writing their girlfriend's name in the yard with the lawnmower when they do decide to mow.

- Maintaining a ransacked room.

- Putting off homework until they want to do it.

- Not wanting to go to bed—and not wanting to get out of it in the morning.

- Texting (SnapChatting, Instagramming, etc.) continually just to stay "connected."

- Not wanting to call anyone to find a job.

- Losing their retainer or contacts, breaking glasses, ripping shirts, ruining shoes.

- Not caring about brushing their teeth but wanting them to be as white as the commercials.

- Not liking who they are and who you are. Wanting everyone else to be like them while they try to be like everyone else.

- Telling you what you want to hear and swearing that nobody listens.

- Forgetting to thank people for gifts they receive.

- Not wanting to go to church.

- Demanding more free time and later curfews and swearing no one else has a curfew.

- Being dissatisfied with any parenting skills you might possess.

- Wanting to be different while trying to be like everyone else.

- Making an occasional bad grade and not caring about making good grades.

- Wanting to be trendy and stylish even when the look might counter what they really believe.

- Not thinking about college until right before (or even after) the application deadline.

- Hating things today they loved yesterday and vice versa—including you.

- Wanting things but not wanting to work for them.

- Not wanting to appear in public with their parents, but wanting parents to finance their public appearances.

- Indulging in occasional outbursts of anger.

- Choosing actions that are more curious and experimental than adoptive and lifelong.

- Not knowing what they want to do as a career.

- Loving music as a means to identify with others rather than because of what it says.

- Saying stupid things that are best left alone and un-noticed.
- Wanting to waste time with friends but feeling like it's a waste of time hanging with Mom and Dad.
- Longing to be told they are loved by someone.
- Wanting security and significance from parents.
- Desiring to get older but never wanting to grow up.

These norms are the nature of the beast called adolescence. The teen years come with their own not-pleasant-to-parents set of behaviors. You do not have to accept and allow all of these, but it should at least relieve you to know almost all teens struggle with these thoughts, behaviors, and feelings.

When to Take a Stand

Some situations are not normal and should immediately prompt you to get your house in order. Some parents allow their teens to slide into situations without realizing the mess they are in until it is so bad the family cannot dig themselves out. This downward slide happens over a long period of time when inappropriate behaviors are gradually accepted. It normally happens slowly. When it all hits the fan, it becomes so overwhelming that some parents, some families, just quit.

I often hear parents justify and excuse potentially dangerous and deadly behaviors. I have to stop them and say, "Let me repeat back to you what you are telling me, and you tell me if you think this is all right." They usually look somewhat aghast as I repeat what I heard them say.

Sometimes parents see only the good in their children. They fail to see what's going wrong and are caught off guard when they realize what is happening.

Let me list some behaviors that demand immediate attention. These behaviors are not normal for teens and are clear indicators you need to get your house in order:

- A sudden change in personality and rejection of normal things.

- New friends, especially association with those you do not want your child to hang around.

- Outbursts of anger that include profanity and show extreme disrespect.

- Extreme need for sleep.

- Depression, including dark thoughts, an inability to get out of bed, sporadic crying for no apparent reason, and ever-increasing risk-taking behaviors.

- Sexual activity.

- Use of drugs, alcohol, or marijuana.

- Getting physical with anyone in the family, including punching, hurting, or beating the family pet.

- Avoidance of any interaction with family and long-time friends.

- Self-injury, including self-mutilation, starvation (anorexia), binging and purging (bulimia), or cutting.

- Failing grades or unwillingness to go to school.

- Rebellion that includes verbal abuse, aggressive behavior, or disrespect for family and friends.

- Dishonesty and disobedience on a regular basis.

- Defiance of the standards of the home and the values of the family.

This is not meant to be an exhaustive list, but these behaviors represent the major areas that indicate the need for prompt correction. In some cases, professional help might be of utmost importance and necessity. Knowing what is normal and what is not can help you determine what you need to focus on in your home and family.

Don't be afraid to do what is right. And don't ever be afraid to ask for help. Your family's survival and your child's life might depend on it.

CHAPTER TEN

DETERMINING RULES AND CONSEQUENCES

*R*ules without relationship cause rebellion, but relationship without rules equals chaos.

One of the great mistakes many parents make is failing to establish a pattern of rules and consequences when their kids are young, so they understand boundaries, good choices, and what happens when their behavior is inappropriate. Such a system is crucial if your home is to operate effectively. Let me explain what I mean and demonstrate the impact such a system can have.

First, the understanding of rules and consequences must be based on your principles and values. This ensures when inappropriate behavior occurs, the consequences are already determined. Kids know the purpose behind the consequences. That is, to uphold your family values and beliefs. Such a system should provide you with a relational policy and procedure manual for your home.

By putting your set of rules and consequences in place and communicating it clearly to your children, you are able to correct mistakes, address new issues when they surface, and get control of situations that can spin or currently are spinning out of control. Early on, you can create an atmosphere where relationships can flourish.

Adolescence often catches a family a little unprepared, causing parents to feel inadequate in managing their home. Organization is crucial during the adolescent years. That is why establishing rules and consequences prior to a child's thirteenth birthday is so important. If that time has come and gone, it is not too late. It just won't be as smooth and easy. If you have never lived out what you believe, creating rules to support those beliefs, establishing consequences for the violation of the rules and communicating these clearly with your children, start today.

Even if you already lined all this out, adolescence calls for updated and renewed rules. Now the kids are old enough for you to enlist their input. What do they think appropriate consequences are for lying, sneaking out, or trying illegal substances? What rewards would they like to receive for practicing good behaviors consistently? When kids are allowed input and feel "ownership" in the system, they are more likely to buy-in to the program. The beginning of difficulties with your teen demands a set of rules that clearly outlines the path you want to follow and the path you don't want to follow. Everyone in the family needs to be on the same page.

Most people do not plan on having problems, so they do not prepare for them. As a result, they have not figured out how to respond until those problems are on top of them. A belief system for your home allows you to prepare for the adolescent years and the challenges and problems they bring. It provides a road map with directions to follow and outlined consequences for getting back on track if anyone in the family gets lost.

Don't misunderstand. This is not a static list of rules that allows you to disconnect from your child by pointing to the refrigerator (where you have your rules posted) when your teen steps out of line. It is a communication tool that gives defined goals, desires, and expectations to your child and backs those up with rules, consequences, and rewards. A belief system communicates to your child, "Let's go this way, and I'll go with you" instead of, "That's the way you need to go, and I'll stand over here and watch."

My son gave me a Father's Day card last year that had an anonymous quote: "The successful man leads where others follow, persists where others give up, speaks softly while others may shout, listens when others may not, and lives from both his head and his heart." I believe by giving this process a little thought and time, developing such a path for your family allows you to live from your head and your heart.

I tell my staff to write down any idea they have about how we should operate Heartlight. Writing down thoughts helps organize them. Soon, you can see a clear path to follow. Writing out your belief system lays out the direction for kids and parents to follow. It also takes the anger and arbitrariness out of discipline.

When there is a set of consequences to follow for certain infractions, your child knows exactly what consequence he is "buying" if he chooses that misbehavior. You don't get caught off guard, reacting in anger because you do not know what to do when you discover an infraction. You just look at the chart and follow the directions you already put in place.

Why is it so important to have things spelled out and not just shoot from the hip? Because teens will question everything you put into play. Knowing your beliefs and values and factoring them into the family system of rules and consequences takes out the guesswork. Your teen might question, but both of you already know the answers. You have a ready response to any of the following challenges your teen may throw down:

"Why?"

"Come on, Dad, that's stupid."

"I am not following those rules."

"Who do you think you are, telling me what to do?"

"Why do we have to do that?"

"You gotta be kidding me!"

"You're not going to tell me how to live."

"What do you mean, *rules?* I have been happy without them."

"Did Mom put you up to this?"

"Who died and made you God?"

"I'll go live with Dad. He doesn't have rules like this!"

"No one else's parent is doing this."

"Come on, Mom, what's the big deal?"

How to Develop Rules and Consequences for Your Home

If your child is spinning out of control and every morning you wake up begging, *Lord, prepare me for whatever is going to happen today*, then you are ripe for establishing a set of rules and consequences for your home. Such a system is vital when you wonder what is next with your teens—whether you will discover they are stealing, using drugs or alcohol again, having sex with their girlfriend or boyfriend, or cutting school today. Many parents of out-of-control kids spend so much time trying to get a handle on all the problems they do not have time to set up a system of rules and consequences, much less think about what they believe.

If you are caught in one of these situations, let me show you how to set up the rules and consequences for your home. This is where the system is most useful. If your home is spinning out, it will help you regain some control.

Begin by asking yourself, *What do I want? What would I like to see changed in my home?* Call it a brainstorming session. Call it a dream. Call it whatever you want, but it is the first step toward getting your house in order.

The best way to answer these questions is to state your beliefs. Your teen will expose them anyway. If your beliefs can stand the scrutiny of adolescence when things are challenged, violated, and complained about, then these truths and beliefs will hold true, and your kids will probably adopt them.

Beliefs About Your Home

Beliefs are convictions, opinions, ideals, morals, and values you hold dear because of your experience, biblical wisdom, tradition, culture, or marriage. If you had to put together a "Top Ten" list of what you believe about your home, what would you write down?

Might I suggest some things to consider that I believe are important? As you go through these, do not think of rules to put with them yet. Just think about what you would like to see.

- Academics: What kind of grades do your kids need to make? Are you going to pay for college? Do your children get to choose where they want to go? Do they have to carry a full load at school? What if they skip class? What if they get in trouble at school? What course of action will you take if they begin to flunk a class?

- Spirituality: Are you going to require your kids to go to church? Do they have to go to Sunday school? Young Life? Camp during the summer? Sunday night church? Wednesday night Bible study? Is there a time they can miss? During their senior year, do you allow them to choose what to do? Do they have to go on the summer mission tour with the church? Do they have to go to your church? What do you do if they hate church? Do they only get to hang out with church kids?

- Social: What kind of curfew are you going to set? When will they be allowed to date? What is that process of dating? Can they stay over at others' homes? Do you have to meet the other parents? What if you disapprove of their friends? Do you have a say in who they may hang out with? Are you going to allow them to hang out at the mall? Will you let them go on the senior trip? How many nights a week can they go out? Do they have to check in during the night? What if they don't come home one night? What if they are late? Do they only group date? Can they go on a trip with the opposite sex?

- Behavior: Are you going to allow disrespect? Do dishonesty and disobedience call for punishment? What is acceptable and unacceptable behavior? Will you allow your kids to drink or smoke? How about pierce or tattoo their bodies? How will you allow them to dress? What do you believe about substances? Drugs? Sex? Will you allow extreme sports like parachuting, bungee jumping, or motocross? What do you believe about teenage pregnancy? What if your child runs away? What if he or she wrecks the car or gets a ticket? What do you think about using the cell phone while driving?

- Character: What character traits would you like to see your children develop? How will you help these grow? How do you want your daughter to present herself in a seductively dressed world, and what will you allow? Do you want your child to have a job? Will sports be required? What kind of work should kids do around the house? How serious is extreme disrespect? What happens when you catch your son in a lie? Who handles the discipline in the family?

- Health: If your child is on medication, are you responsible to make sure it is taken? If you have a special-needs child, how will that affect each family member's responsibilities? What if your children don't take care of their teeth? What if a retainer is lost? Who pays for broken glasses? Who pays for new contacts?

- Possessions: How tidy must your kids' rooms be? Beds made? Where is the computer going to be placed in the home? Who buys the clothes? Who approves of the clothes? What kind of games will you allow? Cell phone? Car? Who pays for these?

- Entertainment: What kind of music will you allow your child to listen to? What ratings of videos and movies are okay? What concerts will you allow them to go to? Which TV programs are okay, and which ones are not? Are you going to allow any entertainment with profanity? What about inappropriate websites? How much social media involvement will you allow?

- Responsibilities: Who's going to do the laundry? Should kids help with meals and cleanup? Who's going to pick up younger siblings from school? How much time needs to be given to help out around the house? Are chores required? What are they? Are you going to give allowance? Will you give more as they get older or less? Who pays car insurance? Who holds the title to the car your kids drive? Will you require your kids to tithe? Do Mom and Dad have a say in where kids work and where they can't? Is it a requirement to work a summer job or part-time job during the year so they have the experience of working for a paycheck and submitting to a boss?

- Privileges: Will you purchase your kids a car when they are sixteen? When do they get to start making choices? Which ones?

- Family: Do you have requirements for family time? How often must the whole family have dinner together? How would you like to see your family members treat one another? Do you need to spell out any blended-family issues?

With so many areas to get a handle on, you may be thankful for birth control. Phew! Did you ever think you would have to consider so much? These are just the questions you know you will have to answer. Who knows what surprises and unexpected challenges you will face in the years ahead?

Perhaps you are not clear about your beliefs and this is why everything seems chaotic and crazy in your home. Why not start now to put things in order? As you do, let me give you just a few other things to consider.

Do Beliefs Change?

Yes, I think beliefs change. Over time, most people change what they believe. I am not talking about shifting with the culture or justifying sinful behavior. Rather, I am suggesting we should make sure we are realistically applying the unchanging truth to our ever-changing lives.

I used to believe some of the following pretty crazy things:

- Toilet seats transmit diseases.
- Vietnam was a good thing.
- Presidents of the United States could never do anything wrong.
- Guys with earrings were gay.
- Rock 'n' roll was evil.
- All Harley riders had scars from gunshot wounds and stabbings.
- All Christians were Republicans.
- California was the land of fruits and nuts.
- If you did all the right things, your child would always do well.
- I could ride anything mechanical or alive.
- My children would always listen to me.
- I'd never be fired from a job.
- I could always trust people.
- A family that prayed together, stayed together.
- Bad things did not happen to good people.
- If I slapped someone on the back while their eyes were crossed, they would stay that way. (My brother still has bruises, and his vision is fine.)

Do beliefs change? You bet they do. So let me ask a tough question: Is what you believe rooted in something that is not right? If it is, you are going to be confronted when you bring it up to your kids. You are going to have some explaining to do. I am not challenging your beliefs, but I want you to be prepared to defend them. What I once thought I would do, I did not. What I promised would happen did not. In many instances, I am glad.

I hear numerous parents state if their teenage daughter ever gets pregnant she would have to leave the house. In more than forty years of working with kids who have gotten pregnant, I have yet to meet a family that followed through on that threat. No dad I know kicked his daughter out of the house because she was pregnant. Rather, I see parents set aside this position so they can help their daughter during her most difficult time.

Without a plan, good intentions fail.

Using an outdated plan to tackle current issues is a disaster in the making. Your beliefs might be in order, but your plan may not. Take time to clarify your primary beliefs and determine whether you have an effective plan for incorporating those beliefs into your family life.

Rick and Vicki

I have performed more than four hundred weddings of kids who lived with us at Heartlight. I have many opportunities to see the long-term effects of what we do. One of the weddings I performed years ago was for a girl named Vicki.

Vicki recently called with some questions about her three teenage sons, ages fourteen, seventeen, and eighteen. The eighteen-year-old lives at home and is attending junior college. Vicki's husband Rick loves the boys dearly and feels the need to have family devotions. He built this desire into the makeup of their home for years.

As the boys moved into their teen years, their mind-set became quite different from their elementary school years. The boys began to question everything. They challenged the style of the devotions. They thought watching children's videos and having discussion time was no longer appropriate.

Their rebellion against Dad's way of doing family devotions caused so much friction in the home the boys began to lose their relationship with father, who had been their best friend. Dad got angrier and angrier as the days passed. He began to lose the enjoyment of being with his three best buds and felt frustrated most of the time as a result of his kids' disrespect. Rick struggled to hear what his sons were telling him, and he had not learned to stop a good thing when it had run its course.

Family devotions can be wonderful. Rick's desire to build eternal perspectives into his kids pleases God. But Rick's approach was wrong. His sons were not learning the way they used to. They longed for something different, and they felt as if they were being treated like little kids. This was a case of great concept but poor delivery. Good belief but bad strategy. Perhaps the family needs a break from the devotions. Maybe the activity could be done a different way. Maybe what was a good idea in early childhood is no longer a good idea in the teen years. If having devotions is destroying relationships, then it is time to evaluate those devotions. Times change. Children grow. So must you.

Pick Your Battles

You could probably come up with a hundred different ways your home could operate differently. But implementing all of those new ideas would overwhelm anyone. Pick a few of the most important items to tackle now and add more later.

I always believed a family should go to church together. When my children grew into their high school years, they did not like the church we were going to, so we decided to go to the church they wanted to attend. That was where all their school friends went. Quite honestly, the church drove me nuts. It was not the place Jan and I felt we should be. We had to choose between going to church as a family and going to churches that were right for each of us.

I shifted. We decided to let them go to their church while we went to ours, and we met for lunch immediately following. Did I no longer believe a family should go to church together? No, I still do. But I could not force our kids to be happy at our church, and I could not force myself to be happy at theirs, so we decided this was not a battle worth fighting.

As I get older, I let go of some of the things I thought were important so I can focus on some wiser truths, more intelligent understandings, and perhaps more sensible beliefs. Sometimes I have gotten stuck in the past, enjoying the way things used to be. That rarely works as family members grow.

Setting the Rules

Once you identify a few beliefs your family can build on, you can formulate rules to help you live out those beliefs. Rules are boundaries that apply the beliefs and define what is acceptable and what is not.

Some teens will be relieved to have rules established, as most young people I meet like knowing the boundaries they can operate within. Others struggle as their parents suddenly erect fences where the kids have been allowed to roam free.

Many parents fail to set the rules of the house because they fear their children's responses. If you are one of those parents, you have a choice to make. You can continue to live in fear of your child, hoping the sense of intimidation you feel will go away, or you can take a stand and face your fear head-on. Remember, behavior can be changed. Your kids may make an initial outburst, but their response will eventually change as you put rules in place and enforce them.

Setting rules draws a line in the sand. If their response is as negative as you anticipate, it will only prove the desperate need for the rules. Of course, this would be one of the first rules for a home like this: Everyone in the family must feel safe and free from emotional outbursts that damage relationships and cause members to live in fear.

The establishment of rules ushers in a time of change and transition. The first response is usually negative, and that is the first change you have to work on. Given time and by offering more to your family, the new rules create a healthier atmosphere where most kids can flourish. Sure, some teens flounder a bit, but do not let that keep you from creating a healthy family environment. Everyone can adjust. Everyone can adapt.

People often ask me what happens when children will not adapt to the new system, and their negative and inappropriate behavior escalates. My answer is simple: The child cannot continue to live at home. Why? Because no one person is more important than the whole family. To allow one person to remain in the home who is willfully and deliberately destroying the family or himself is a great disservice to others in the home.

When you let children know you will not allow them to continue such behavior, you make a critical statement: This family is worth fighting for, and nothing will stand between us that keeps us from moving where God desires us to be.

Establishing Consequences

Now that you have established the rules, you need to set consequences in place. Consequences are actions applied to the breaking of the rules you have established. Consequences are not just a way to punish negative behavior. They are designed to direct your child toward a better life.

Consequences can be the loss of various things such as the following:

- Participation in certain activities (nights out, prom, date night, movie night, youth group)

- Anything electronic (computer, cell phone, Internet, TV)

- Privileges (use of car, freedom to stay up later, boat, family property)

- Items a parent may provide (car insurance, vacation, a home, gas money, allowance)

- A work project, duty, or extra chores.

The reason for establishing consequences is to keep your children from behaving a particular way, not simply to punish them for wrongdoing. Focus on correction more than justice, direction more than punishment, and guidance more than retribution. The reason for establishing a belief system is to determine the path your children should take and to keep them from dark places where they do not want to be. Consequences are more than retribution kids should receive for doing something wrong or unacceptable.

Think of consequences as course correctors.

Begin by prioritizing your beliefs and rules. Match the greatest consequences to the highest priorities. If you consider academics to be the highest priority for your child, then tie the toughest consequence to poor academic performance. For instance, if your children love being on the computer more than anything in the world, take away their computer privileges for a couple of weeks as the consequence for not passing all their classes.

Personally, my big issues with kids are respect, obedience, and honesty. The toughest consequences would be attached to any violation of those. I would focus on behaviors like drug or alcohol use, driving under the influence, and physical issues like violence or sexual promiscuity.

Allow me to take the areas I listed earlier and set some rules for each, with corresponding consequences. This will give you an idea of what a belief system might look like. Let me encourage you to come up with your own rules and consequences to fit your children, their ages, and their situations, all based on what you desire to accomplish within your family. Again, see if your children will contribute to this family system. I list items here just to give you an idea of how this could look. Please do not take the following comments as directives. I repeat: This is only an example.

Academics

Belief: Our children should be able to pass all their classes throughout their high school years.

Rule: There will be no failing grades in school.

Consequence: No computer time at home other than for homework until all grades are passing grades.

Spirituality

Belief: Our children will attend church or some other resource for spiritual input.

Rule: Our children will attend church once a week.

Consequence: Loss of a weekend night out.

Social

Belief: Nothing good happens after midnight.

Rule: Curfew is midnight on weekends.

Consequence: Loss of allowance for two weeks.

Behavior

Belief: Each family member should be treated with respect.

Rule: All family members will treat each other with the utmost respect.

Consequence: First offense: grounding for one week, which includes the loss of all privileges except attendance at school and job responsibilities. Repeated offenses: grounding for two-week periods with loss of the car and loss of allowance. If this grounding is not effective, the car will be sold or computer given away.

Character

Belief: Family members should strive to improve their character.

Rule: Each family member will have breakfast with either Mom or Dad once a week to talk about life issues and discuss the future. In addition, one week every summer will be devoted to working on a mission project somewhere.

Consequence: No Saturday night out.

Health

Belief: Every family member should follow any medical advice.

Rule: Everyone in this family will take all prescribed medicine.

Consequence: iPods, TV, and other electrical devices in the house will be left off.

Possessions

Belief: Bedrooms should be cleaned regularly.

Rule: A messy room is okay throughout the week, but it must be cleaned every weekend. Cleaning includes dusting, vacuuming, and picking up anything that does not belong on the floor.

Consequence: Loss of allowance for one week.

Entertainment

Belief: R-rated movies should not be seen.

Rule: R-rated movies will be allowed only if approved by Mom. Notice must be given to her a few days in advance.

Consequence: Loss of TV or going to the movies for a month and the poking out of one eye (just kidding).

Responsibilities

Belief: Teenagers should be able to do their own laundry.

Rule: Each person will wash, fold, and put away his or her laundry each week.

Consequence: Soiled clothes will be confiscated and can be purchased back from Mom.

Privileges

Belief: Family members should know where everyone is at all times.

Rule: When there is a change of plans, the cell phone provided should be used to call and advise of the change.

Consequence: A four-hour work project.

Family

Belief: The family should have at least one night a week together.

Rule: The entire family will eat dinner together and enjoy an activity every Monday night.

Consequence: No inheritance (also a joke). Two family nights the week after one is missed.

I have learned a few invaluable lessons about rules through the years. One is to use humor. Humor always makes a pill a little easier to swallow. Most young people will feel a little constrained by their family's belief system, but with a little humor, they tend to respond more positively.

Also, rules without relationship cause rebellion.

If you do not have good relationships with your children, they will view rules as herd management or your way of avoiding frustration. If you do not have solid relationships, let your children know your desire to build them. Add extra time together to the relational side of the belief system, like a trip somewhere or twice-weekly parent/child time together.

Believe it or not, young people want rules. They want to know what is expected and what is not. Kids feel freer when they know where the boundaries are. They want to know what is important to Mom and Dad and when they get to make their own choices. We require all the families at Heartlight to put together a system of rules and consequences for their homes before their children return. I often laugh because the children usually come up with harder rules than the parents do! The children in our program understand a set of expectations and clearly defined directives helps relationships flourish. Deep down, the kids desire to have a relationship with Mom and Dad.

Wouldn't that be nice? To have a child who really wants a relationship with you? By establishing a belief system, you help make that possible, especially if you have lost the connection with your child somewhere along the way. Once your system is in place, you can allow some things to happen that we discussed in the first half of the book—allowing pain to enter the picture and helping your child begin to understand the concept of consequences.

You are now allowing your children the opportunity to flourish as they have the freedom to choose success or failure. Sure, their clothes are going to be all pink a couple times as they learn to do their own laundry; but as they accept changes and take on some new responsibilities, they will learn it is time to grow up. Not an easy thing for a Mom or Dad to watch. But in time, the system of rules and consequences you craft for your family will yield great benefits.

CHAPTER ELEVEN

SETTING BOUNDARIES

an and I had just returned home. The moment we walked into our home I felt like one of the three bears who knew someone ate his food, slept in his bed, and sat in his chair. I had a sneaking suspicion our son Adam had been up to something while we were on vacation.

Just the weekend before, we visited Texas Tech with Adam to look at the school. After spending some time there, he decided it was not the place because he did not see enough trees, and he saw too much alcohol. I supported his decision and was impressed that he based his choice on a couple of good principles. (Yes, I was born in Midland, Texas, where people dream of tall pines and fall foliage!)

When we got back from our college visit, Jan and I got ready to go on a little vacation by ourselves. We let Adam know that while we were gone, we would trust him. No one was to come over or spend the night, and he was to take care of the house, dogs, and any problems that came up. We felt confident he could handle the responsibilities. Shoot, he better be able to—he was going off to college in a few months!

Upon our return, I walked in the door and noticed dirt on the floor. Food was gone, beds were messed up, and our bathroom tub had been used. A feeling of uneasiness ruined the relaxing effects of our vacation. I asked Adam if anything happened while we were gone.

Adam said, "Nope, nothing happened. I will get everything cleaned up."

I still felt like Papa Bear of the Three Bears coming home and knowing something just was not right. Later that night, I went up to his room and asked again, "You sure nothing happened here while we were gone?"

"I am sure, Dad," he replied.

I thought to myself, *I know I was born at night, but I was not born* last *night*. I have had kids lying to me almost all my adult life, and my son suddenly showed all the symptoms of one who was lying through his teeth. I knew something went on, and I was now on a mission to find out what it was.

The next day I decided to mow the lawn. Riding the mower around gives me time to think. I came upon a few dozen beer bottle caps, and immediately thought I should call the local airline for dumping the waste from their plane in my yard. When

Adam got home from school, I told him about the airline dumping the beer bottle caps and that I was going to file a complaint.

He could no longer hide his guilt and embarrassment. "Dad, something did go on while you guys were gone."

I asked, "Really? What?"

He replied, "I wish I could tell you, but I don't remember." He had been a little too tanked to know what happened. While he was blitzed, some other guys took advantage of the situation.

Beer, wine coolers, cigars, girls, and partying filled our house and drained my confidence that Adam had developed some good principles to live by. He apologized, and we grounded him for a while. Not much else you can do to an eighteen-year-old who is headed off to college.

You know what bothered me the most? It was not the fact that he violated our rules of the house, nor was it the experimentation with beer, wine coolers, and cigars. It was not that he went against what we asked. It was not that he did neglected the responsibilities we gave him. It was not that others sneaked around behind our backs. And it was not that an airline dumped beer bottle caps in our yard.

What bothered me most was the personal violation I felt. Adam walked all over our boundaries and tried to cover up his actions. His disrespect made his apologies feel a little hollow.

It's All About Respect

The belief system we discussed in the last chapter is vital to getting your house in order. It is a big step in the right direction. This chapter is about your need to set boundaries for yourself, your home, and your family. These boundaries are not about how to run your home; they are about respecting you as the parent.

As you read in the last chapter, I believe respect is the main issue in any home. If children do not develop the character trait of respect, a belief system will not bring transformation. Without a sense of respect for others, children will not create meaningful relationships or succeed in life. By creating boundaries for your own life and home, and by teaching your children to respect those boundaries, you can restore or enhance your relationship with your children.

I know of a couple that moved hundreds of miles away from their grown kids so they could live with boundaries in their lives. They gave up their friends, their church, and their beautiful home and moved far away to start over. They just could not get their grown kids to respect their boundaries, so they went looking for a place where they would be respected. A little disrespect from your children now can threaten to ruin your life later.

Perhaps you know those feelings because you have been violated by your teen. Do any of these feel familiar?

- You feel walked on.
- You feel forced to do things you don't want to do.
- You are treated shamefully by your kids.

- Your life has revolved around them for years.

- You have no life, no outlet, and you are going crazy.

- Your kids dump on you, take it out on you, and beat you up verbally.

- Your teen has gotten physically violent.

- You are at your kids' beck and call all the time.

- You feel emotionally and psychologically violated.

- You are lied to, deceived, and manipulated.

Sounds like the makings of a good country song, doesn't it? But these feelings are real, and they can make you want to run, regardless of how good your belief system looks on paper. Every belief system is only as powerful as the person behind it. It is simply a tool parents can use to guide their children.

When It Is About You

My encouragement to you as a parent is to set some boundaries that are about you. Choose boundaries to help you be the person God calls you to be in your family. This is the place in this book where it is about you. It is about your ability to lead your family to a place of respect, order, and relationship. If you are going to steer this herd, you have to take care of *you*!

The power and authority you possess determine the strength of the rules, beliefs, and requirements you set within your home. Without your child's respect, rules mean nothing. Your children must learn to respect you in your decisions, whether they agree or not. Respect you as a person. Respect your limits.

And respect your boundaries, regardless of how absurd they might think they are.

What Are Boundaries?

Boundaries are the parameters or fences that define our own space. They describe what is ours and what is not. They may include locks on doors; words that reflect our personal desires; or rules, standards, and principles by which we choose to live. They make distinctions between what is off-limits and what is okay for you.

Boundaries allow you to establish your priorities. They let the fruit of self-control grow in your life. They give you a sense of backbone and confidence so no one can walk on you. They define who you are and who you are not.

Henry Cloud and John Townsend, authors of the best-selling classic *Boundaries*, offer this clarification: "Boundaries define us. They define what is me and what is not me. A boundary shows me where I end and someone else begins, leading me to a sense of ownership."[1]

The Parenting Shift

As our children grow, we must shift our style of parenting. We transition from provision, which is appropriate for children in their elementary school years, to preparation, which helps young people become mature and responsible. Sadly, rather than strategically planning this transition, most parents wait until conflict forces the shift.

The transition works best when it is clearly defined beforehand. It should send a message to your children that says, "The way we have operated is changing, and there are new expectations, new boundaries, and new responsibilities."

The Jewish community celebrates this transition with a bat mitzvah for girls and a bar mitzvah for boys. In these formal ceremonies, the family and community recognize children are entering adulthood. The events highlight the onset of this important transition. These ceremonies are marked by celebration, merriment, gift-giving, blessings, and honoring the teen. Unfortunately for many Gentile families, this transition is a time of strife, confusion, and distress. It does not have to be that way.

Let me make a suggestion. When your children reach adolescence—I would choose age thirteen—create a special time when you formally recognize the transition to more responsibility and maturity. Mark a change in the way you relate to them. Let them know they are no longer children; now you will treat them as young adults. If you do not make the shift proactively, you will more than likely be forced to make the shift reactively at a point of conflict.

Here are some needed parental shifts:

- From teaching to training.
- From endless lecture to engaging discussion.
- From instilling character to shaping character.
- From providing to preparing.
- From control to guidance and counsel.

- From dependence to independence.

- From your answers to their questions.

- From complete caretaking to responsibility.

- From allowing immaturity to demanding maturity.

The parenting style that worked for you in elementary school will not work during the middle school and junior high years. What works for you in the middle school and junior high years will not work for you in the high school years. What works in high school will not work in the college years. As your kids grow, they will think your previous parenting style is childish. Too many parents do not shift the way they parent as their children grow. They end up provoking their children, who become frustrated, irritated, and aggravated.

If your teens still …

dig through your purse,

walk into your bathroom unannounced,

refuse to clean up after themselves,

act as if no one else lives in the house,

yell and scream at you,

demand you do things the way you always have,

refuse to help around the house,

emotionally dump on you whenever there is a problem,

make demeaning and arrogant comments to you and about you,

and require you to be their servants …

you have a problem! It is not a problem with your teens. It is a problem with your boundaries.

Clearly, in your children's minds the shift did not happen. Perhaps it did not happen in yours. It will not occur naturally. You must make it happen. If you do not do it willingly now, you may be forced to do so because of a crisis.

Responses to Boundaries

If you present new boundaries and new responsibilities with celebration and festivity, your kids are likely to receive those boundaries as gifts. When new boundaries and responsibilities are given as a result of conflict and crisis, kids feel restricted and limited at a time when they believe they should be given more freedom and greater independence.

The most effective way to handle the shift is to build a tradition in your family that marks the age of thirteen as the beginning of adulthood. If your kids are under thirteen, now is a good time to build this concept into your belief system so your family can look forward to that time and celebrate it. If your child is older and you missed the opportunity to acknowledge this transition, look for a time to make this transition official. Allow your child's next birthday to usher in a new way of thinking and new expectations.

Leslie

When Leslie came to us, she was spinning out of control. She was drinking, partying, skipping school, and involved sexually with a young man. She hated everything and was out to prove her dislike for the world and everyone in it. She was not exactly the most enjoyable teen to be around.

She openly expressed her hatred of her dad. She made it clear she thought he was a wimp. She felt he always treated her like a little girl, and he needed her a lot more than she needed him. She felt the same way about her mom. Her mother was always smothering her, never giving her any space to breathe, and always wanting to be there for her. She felt Mom also treated her as if she was a small child.

Leslie's dad told me, "I gave up all hope of ever having a relationship with her. For a few years, our eyes rarely made contact except to exchange angry glances. She is a confused little girl who shared nothing but hatred for me. I once told her I never wanted to see her again."

Her mom shared that her little princess turned into a witch, and she now could not stand to be around the daughter she loved so much.

As Leslie's mom and dad poured out their hearts, I thought to myself, *What a mess.* I even questioned whether I really wanted to dive in and help them get out of this whirlpool of a lost teen. I really did not see much hope. I saw a father who gave up on his daughter, a mother who was broken and lost, and a daughter who did not care about anyone or anything, especially her parents.

After months of conversations, counseling, observations, and cups of coffee, I finally realized why this family did not have any boundaries. It was because of the position they gave Leslie. These parents used to idolize their daughter. Setting boundaries around someone you idolize is almost impossible.

Leslie was their pride and joy. They lived their life for her and worshipped her. No child could live up to those expectations. Leslie's behavior was designed to prove to them she was not perfect and to send the message she was not going to allow them to put her on a pedestal anymore.

This young lady was actually establishing her own boundaries. She was not doing it in the best of ways, but her intention was to create her own identity and break away from the "fantasy Leslie" her parents created.

Mom and Dad needed to let her go, let her grow up, and start acting like a mom and dad. Leslie needed to become a daughter with boundaries and stop being a goddess who could do no wrong.

My first task was to help Leslie's parents take her off the pedestal. The second task was to help them put some boundaries in place that would define and protect the positions each person holds in their family.

Leslie's dad later stated, "You helped us grow as parents and recognize and embrace the hurt, frustrated, and angry adolescents *we* still were inside. That not only helped us but also helped Leslie as we went through the process of self-discovery."

Leslie's mom shared that she began to realize she needed to take her children off their pedestals and set boundaries within the home, so everyone could flourish and grow. Leslie had to learn to love and be loved in a new way. Boundaries helped get their situation under control.

Candice

Candice was a fourteen-year-old girl whose mom coddled her most of her life. Her mother never established boundaries because of the guilt she felt from a divorce when Candice was five and her consequent need to have a close relationship with her daughter. Their relationship was more of peers or friends than parent and child. Now Candice was out of control. Her mother knew it but felt helpless.

Candice was one of those girls I really did not like when I first met her. She would break things and not show any remorse. She believed anything she did wrong was someone else's fault. She would walk right into the bathroom when it was occupied. She would yell and scream at anyone at any time for any reason. She was volatile, and people went out of their way to avoid her. She borrowed other girls' things without asking. When confronted about the way she treated someone, she would immediately say she was sorry, but it was not sincere. Then she would use her apology to go no further in restoring relationship, stating, "I said I am sorry. What else do you want me to do?"

I decided the best way to approach Candice was to put one boundary before her. I expected her to act her age, and I would treat her the same. Most of the time, I felt like I was correcting a five-year-old who had the mouth of a twenty-five-year-old. That needed to change.

Not surprisingly, her response to my suggestion was horrible because my approach limited her ability to act the way she did. She not only rejected limits, restrictions, and boundaries, she hated them. The first time I confronted her, she walked into her house and shaved her head. About an hour later, she came out to show me what she had done. She left a single inch-wide strip of hair, six inches long, on the front of her head. She was out to get me and express her frustration. She was telling me I just violated one of her boundaries, and she was going to show me I would not get away with that.

I told her she looked good with no hair—not a comment she wanted to hear. Just before she stormed off, I told her she was now getting a taste of how it felt to have her boundaries crossed. It made her even more mad, and her anger increased over the next few months.

My heart aches when I see young people stick to their guns and hold onto their damanging, dangerous lifestyles because they fear impending change. Candice's stubbornness kept her in a painful place for a long time. But her anger also gave us a flicker of hope. Remember, anger is like a dashboard warning light. The signal Candice gave when she was mad showed us we were getting closer to the issues she was harboring.

We had one confrontation after another, one fight after another, one long emotional draining interaction after another.

But as we taught, fought, confronted, loved on, and spent time with Candice—and as the other kids at Heartlight shared with her in group therapy meetings what they saw in her—she began to realize she was separated and isolated from relationships because of her unwillingness to respect other people's boundaries. She eventually began to see how she really acted. Because what she saw was so ugly, Candice ran the other direction. Her response was not perfect, but she was at least willing to change for the better.

My purpose in sharing Candice's story is to help prepare you for a struggle when you first place boundaries on kids. It is like putting a bridle on a horse that ran free for years. Be prepared for the response and possible reaction. The fight is usually long and hard. The earlier you can begin the process, the better.

Do Boundaries Always Work?

People often ask if this "boundary thing" always works. The answer is no. Some kids just will not accept boundaries. Young men usually want independence and often react against restrictions. Young ladies, on the other hand, want intimacy, which is usually found through relationships developed in social circles. They are so relational that when you begin to restrict social gatherings and social interactions, you might get a pretty strong reaction. For example, a girl may fly off the handle if she is kept from going to the prom because of inappropriate behavior.

When boundaries are determined early, children get used to the authority of parents. They learn the ropes of relationships and discover the fences of appropriate behavior. On the other hand, imposing new boundaries on older teens is a disaster waiting to happen. It is like allowing a boy to drive at age sixteen and then taking away his license until he is seventeen. Your teens will probably respond a little more intensely if they have already tasted freedom and you try to take it away.

So what's the point? Again, if you have the chance, set the boundaries early. If you are just now trying to set boundaries with older teens, expect a fight as you implement them. That does not mean your boundaries are wrong. It does not mean give up. It just means be prepared. Remember, kids' reactions to boundaries are not indicators of the boundaries' appropriateness.

Quite honestly, I see some horses I just can't break. They are too old, have too many habits, or are too used to not being handled. Unless you are a horse whisperer with a ton of experience, chances are the older ones will not accept a bridle.

At that point, a parent has a choice to make. You can allow your child to remain at home, then batten down the hatches and prepare for stormy weather. Or you can send your child to a place like Heartlight, where we can reach kids with the same boundaries they might reject from their parents. (We did not give them the freedoms they enjoy, so the reaction is not as personal when we take them away. Plus, when they are brought to us, they can no longer live at home and have no place else to go. It is literally our way or the highway.)

Some kids who never respond to boundaries at home eventually learn those boundaries in the workplace, in a college setting, or in a marriage. Some even learn boundaries for themselves when they have their own children. Unfortunately, they will more than likely get fired a few times, kicked out of school, or even lose a marriage in the process of learning boundaries a little too late to save some situations.

Respecting Your Boundaries

As I wrote earlier, a belief system helps get your house in order. Setting boundaries helps you get your belief system in order. Setting boundaries for yourself tells your children, "This is who I am," "This is who we are," and "This is what our home will be like."

Nothing is wrong with letting people know what you want and asking them to respect your wishes. It is okay to expect kids to knock on the door, leave others' things alone unless they ask, drive your car only with your permission, stay out of your room and bathroom, and borrow your clothes only if you say yes. It is okay to have your own space.

Establishing boundaries empowers you. It also allows your children to make decisions and choose consequences in volatile situations. You set the boundaries and rules, and your children decide whether they are going to follow or break those rules, thus choosing their own rewards or consequences.

As your child moves into the teen years, you can put to rest some old habits, routines, and practices. Slamming doors.

Watching cartoons on Saturday morning. Sleeping late on certain mornings. The way you interact as a family. Be willing to set boundaries to put a stop to certain habits and behaviors that are no longer acceptable.

When we first started Heartlight, our family lived in one room for two-and-a-half years. It was so cramped that each night we had to rotate from the bed to the sofa to the floor. We only had one bed that slept two. My son was in third grade. My daughter was in seventh. One morning my daughter Melissa was taking her frustrations out on my wife Jan. To make a long story short, I intervened when the verbal barrage got out of hand and Melissa acted disrespectful.

I walked into the bathroom where they were verbally duking it out, put my finger on my daughter, looked her straight in the eye and said firmly, "You will not treat my wife like this anymore. Understand?" Our daughter got the message loud and clear. I established a boundary and helped my wife remember she was worthy of respect.

You can set boundaries around your time too. Driving kids to school, sports events, church events, and social activities takes time. Being involved in your kids' schoolwork takes time. Shopping, cleaning, fixing, helping … no wonder many parents struggle when their kids go to college; they never had time to build a life of their own.

Sometimes it is okay to say, "I can't do that," and allow your child to go it alone. It is okay to have some personal time. And it is okay to say no to something because you would rather do something else. Your behavior teaches kids to do the same. Your mentoring in this area shows them the value of boundaries and helps them understand the need to set them in their own life as well.

Respect Their Boundaries

As your teens see your boundaries, they learn to develop boundaries for themselves. Because of their selfish nature, their quest for independence, and their desire to make decisions on their own, they will not want you to meddle in their personal affairs. As a parent, you still need to determine what is appropriate and not appropriate. While kids need to respect all of your boundaries, your goal is to respect as many of theirs as you can, while keeping them healthy and safe.

The older teens get, the more decisions they should make for themselves. Children will set some boundaries for themselves you should respect, and you will set boundaries for them they must respect. Generally, if your kids' boundaries violate your family's beliefs and rules, you may need to violate any unhealthy boundaries.

Of course, tell your kids beforehand. Tell them about the software on the computer that monitors every place they go and every word they type. Tell them you respect their privacy, but you will also do whatever is necessary to determine if they are participating in something unacceptable in your home. It is not because you want to play policeman or feel you have to control everything. Let them know your inquisitiveness helps you learn to trust them so they can take control of their own lives. By checking periodically, let them know you do not always have to be on guard about their every move.

The Stage Is Set

I spoke at a church not too long ago that had one of the most fantastic youth buildings I ever saw. It cost four million dollars, and it was designed to create an environment attractive to teens. It helped them feel valuable and created new opportunities for ministry. I was in awe as I saw how much this church valued its youth.

The room I was to speak in was gorgeous. The lighting was fantastic, the sound system was crisp, the air conditioning was perfect. The setup was superb, and all the planning brought a large crowd. Anticipation filled the air.

Then I walked up to speak.

When I got up front, I noticed (as did everyone else) the lighting was aimed somewhere other than where I was standing. About five minutes after I began, the batteries in the microphone went dead. A little later, the air conditioning—which was on an electrical timer—quit.

What seemed a perfect setting by all appearances quickly became dim, hot, and silent. Before long I was standing in the dark, sweating and yelling. Even then, not everyone could hear me. Something well-planned and so well set up became a disaster in the space of an hour. The reason soon became evident: The person in charge thought everything was okay, so he left.

That evening reinforced for me some important lessons. First, never assume everything will remain okay. As you put together a belief system for your home and set boundaries, remain engaged with your family. Do not assume the system will take care of itself. As time passes, you will discover areas that need adjustment and attention.

Second, regardless of how beautiful your system may appear, it will never run on its own. It takes your *constant* involvement. When God told Joshua to cross the Jordan River and enter the Promised Land, He added, "I will never leave you nor forsake you" (Joshua 1:5).

This same message must be communicated to our teens, especially during times of struggle and difficulty. A system will not fix anything on its own. A system within the context of relationships can lead a child into right standing with those who love him.

Once the stage is set, do not leave. Stay engaged. You never know when an airline is going to dump beer bottle caps in your yard.

CHAPTER TWELVE

ALLOWING YOUR CHILD TO BE IN CONTROL

God called you to an incredibly challenging role as a parent. However, your hope and confidence can continue to grow as you discover and apply principles to help you get your children where they need to be.

In all the challenges you face as a parent, never lose sight of the primary role God called you to as a mom or dad: to lead your children from total dependency at birth to independence by the end of their teenage years.

As we have seen, your parenting style will shift as your child ages. These shifts must occur in sync with your child's maturation process; otherwise, your children end up frustrated because they either want more freedom or are not prepared to handle life's challenges.

The various stages of parenting are simple. Knowing when to move from one stage to the next is much more difficult. Poor timing can lead to rebellion, frustration, and confusion.

The Four P's of Parenting

There is a progression in parenting that can be immensely valuable as you lead your child to independence. The stages overlap, but clarifying parents' changing roles can be helpful.

Stage One: Pleasing Your Child

From a child's birth through the preschool years, the parents' primary role is to please their child. They do that by offering relief from pain, unhappiness, and sickness.

Nobody enjoys a baby who is colicky or fussy. Everyone loves a baby who sleeps through the night. A good baby is a happy baby. If a baby cries, parents do whatever they can to quiet him. If he is fussy, parents try to figure out what is bothering him and do whatever they can to soothe him. No wonder these little kids feel like the center of their parents' world. They are!

In this first stage of pleasing your child, you have total control.

Stage Two: Protecting Your Child

When our children are in their toddler through elementary years, they would probably accidentally kill themselves if we were not around to protect them. Parents keep young children from dangerous and inappropriate activities and influences in this stage.

When boys' thrill of adventure exceeds their understanding of safety, parents worry about them getting hurt in sports, on the playground, on their bikes, climbing trees, or just clowning around. Parents also do not want their children to suffer rejection or be exposed to anything violent, sexual, or immoral.

In this second stage, parents maintain control.

Stage Three: Providing for Your Child

The third stage of parenting is providing for your child. This stage usually begins in the junior high years. We begin to give our junior high children experiences, possessions, and opportunities far greater than we gave them in the elementary years. We allow them to spread their wings a little, and we begin to expose them to the world outside the home.

At this stage, others begin to coach, teach, instruct, train, tutor, mentor, and educate our kids. Our children begin to get serious about sports, music, and academics. They also begin to go to youth group, Bible studies, mission trips, ski trips, overnighters, slumber parties, and organized sports and school activities. They may take a school trip, and we begin to trust others to take care of our children.

We also begin to teach our kids responsibility and trust them to start making some decisions. They may learn to wake up to an alarm, take care of a pet, perform certain chores around the house, and learn to cook simple meals.

In this third stage, we start to share some control.

Stage Four: Preparing Your Child

The fourth stage of parenting usually begins during the high school years, when a child prepares to move out of the nest and into a new life outside of the home.

This is when you begin to hand over control. It is also the stage when we feel like we are losing control. The truth of the matter is that we are. We can give control of our children's lives to them in appropriate ways, so they can function independently by the time they leave home. Or they can wrest it from us with inappropriate behavior.

In this stage, we want to give our children control.

Good Intentions Are Not Enough

I am often asked by puzzled parents, "How can something so well-intentioned go so wrong?"

It is another good question, easy to answer when you understand the concept of free will. But the real issue for most parents is whether they were led astray or did something wrong without knowing it. Without question I believe some parents were led astray and, as a result, messed up. When parents are desperate for answers for their children, they sometimes listen to anything.

Some well-meaning parents get stuck at a certain stage of parenting because they do not know what lies ahead, they do not recognize the need to move to the next stage, or they do not understand that decisions and habits developed during one stage must shift when moving to the next.

For example, if parents do not shift away from always pleasing their children, they get trouble when their kids move to seventh and eighth grades. If parents never move out of the protective stage and let their kids taste the outside world, by the high school years neither the child nor the parents function well. If parents never prepare kids during the high school years for the world ahead, disorder and confusion surround these young adults in their college years. Sometimes provision in one stage becomes enabling in another, even with the best intentions.

Furthermore, if parents do not let go of the major emphasis of each stage of parenting by the time kids are in high school, they create a real mess. If parents still try to please at all cost, strive to protect in every circumstance, and struggle to make sure they constantly provide all their children's needs, they create a muddled, mixed-up, chaotic atmosphere. Their children will act out because they feel insecure and unprepared to enter the world, or they act frustrated because they cannot get out of the environment they have outgrown.

More Perspective on Homeschooling

Some Christian teens pay a great price for parents who have hearts to protect their children. This sometimes comes with homeschooling, setting high standards, placing tight boundaries, and preventing exposure to anything that challenges the family's beliefs. Let me state this again: I am not against homeschooling, standards, boundaries, and protection. However, I also believe we must prepare our children to function well in the world in which they will eventually live. They are not to be of the world, but they need to know how to live in it.

Our residential counseling program works with kids who are struggling. These kids are no different from yours and mine. Most were raised in Christian homes. Many of the kids who come to us were homeschooled, raised with the highest standards, and kept away from anything remotely non-Christian. What I hear most from these kids is this: "My parents are over-protective," "They have high standards no one can live up to," and "They won't let me do anything."

Time and time again, these kids tell me the others they associate with in their homeschool programs are socially isolated and inept. Do I believe only dorky kids are homeschooled? No. There are dorks in every school. But I do believe a lack of inter-action, for some children, prevents them from learning to function well socially.

Many times I have seen homeschooled kids really struggle when they are sent off to public school in the high school years. The guys are ridiculed, and the girls are exploited. When parents hear what is happening, they are even more convinced they need to homeschool their children. They do not realize the way they homeschooled may be part of the problem.

People are shocked when I tell them one of the largest groups of kids at Heartlight are those who homeschooled beyond the eighth grade. Again, I am not against homeschooling or protecting our kids. As mentioned earlier, we homeschool all sixty kids at Heartlight.

However, if your schooling, whether public, private, or homeschooling, does not include the opportunity for your child to make decisions, formulate choices, and experience small bits of social hurt, conflict, and rejection, you are just postponing the inevitable. The longer you wait, the harder it will hit your child, and the pain can be more than many adults can handle. I am not just talking about socialization issues. I am including developmental opportunities and peer integration needs. Your children need to learn to make choices.

You do not want your son to make a decision to smoke pot with his new friends solely because he desperately wants to fit in. You do not want your beautiful daughter to engage in sexual activity for the first time because a hormone-laden young man convinced her he can help her fit in socially.

If your children homeschool, they need opportunities to mix with those who disagree with them and are different from them. They need to make decisions within that context. Limited amounts of social hurt, conflict, and rejection create opportunities for parents to impart wisdom in the midst of the pain, thus preparing teens for what they will experience later in life.

Many parents ask me how long a child should be homeschooled. My answer is this: As long as you want. But sometime during the elementary years, I encourage you to allow your child to experience a little of what you protected her from. If you do, your child will be better prepared to enter the culture.

Remember, your children were created for relationships. With you, yes. With God, absolutely. But also with others their own age. You instill a sense of value in your children, but that value is authenticated by their peers. The acceptance by peers helps move your children into the current of society and prevent them from fearing the world they were created to live in.

Allowing your homeschooled children to interact with and experience some of the things you protected them from needs to continue into and beyond the seventh- and eighth-grade years. At this age, kids begin to practice what they learned— outside the protective shield of homeschooling.

Mark Twain in *A Tramp Abroad* said it best: "The most permanent lessons in morals are those which come, not of booky teaching, but of experience."[1] If you have not made this transition to letting your children experience some of the world so they can better prepare for what is to come, I want you to know it is never too late. You may need to create a strategy to help your children catch up that will not overwhelm them. Talk with your child so he knows and understands the process.

Let me assure you, exposure to the world makes for some pretty interesting discussions. And it can reinforce kids' desire for a relationship with Christ as they grasp His love for the world and see the world's need.

Transferring Control

If you realize you are overly controlling, shift some of that control to your child. You may control because your family lacks boundaries and a belief system to help kids make healthy decisions. As a result, your child may be immature and irresponsible. If you do not know if you are too controlling, take a break from reading for a minute. Text your child and ask, "Do you think we are over-controlling parents?" You do not have to thank me for the lively discussion at the dinner table tonight!

When I make this statement to parents, they often reply, "My daughter is immature and irresponsible. You want me to transfer control to her? You've got to be kidding!"

If that's what you think, let me give you some important perspective. First, he who is faithful in little is faithful in much. If you wait to transfer control until your children are successful at displaying maturity and responsibility, you thwart their maturation. You give a little control because that is what your child needs, not because your child deserves it. If you gave your children what they really deserved, they would probably never be able to leave home! Transferring control before you and your teen are struggling is always best.

Overly controlled children are raised with the best of intentions. They usually have loving parents who are trying to protect them from making mistakes, trying to keep them from being exposed to harmful influences outside the home, or trying to keep them from failure. Dr. Henry Cloud states, "Over-controlled children are subject to dependency, enmeshment conflicts, and difficulty setting and keeping firm boundaries. They also have problems taking risks and being creative."[2]

Anna

I was teaching a seminar in Richmond, Va., when a young mother shared with me during lunch that she thought her fourteen-year-old daughter Anna had reactive attachment disorder. She shared that her daughter was very disrespectful at home. She always rolled her eyes, cussed, yelled, and screamed at her parents. She was verbally aggressive and insolent.

When I asked more about Anna, I found she was adopted from Korea when she was eight. She was now homeschooled after two years in the public school system. The home intentionally had no TV, no Internet access, no privileges to talk on the phone, and no opportunity to play any type of sports.

The parents allowed Anna to go to church and to a small group that met once a week. They also boarded a horse for Anna and her younger brother, and allowed each of the kids to have their own dog. Other people at church loved Anna and thought she was a wonderful young lady. The small group leader loved having Anna in her group.

After an hour-and-a-half discussion, Anna's mom finally asked me, "Do you think this is about us?"

I hesitated to answer. I do not have a problem sharing the truth with parents about what I observe, but I was moved by this lady's passion for her daughter. I did not want her to give up doing good things for Anna.

Before I could answer, she said, "It is about us, isn't it?"

I said, "Yeah, it sounds like it." We talked for a couple of hours about why Anna does what she does, the impact of her adoption, issues surrounding the losses Anna experienced, and what drove Anna's issue with control. I eventually agreed with Anna's mom that Anna had symptoms of RAD.

However, I also saw a problem with that conclusion. Anna was only reactive to her parents, and they seemed to be the only people she was not attached to. This disorder is not usually selective. I finally concluded her reactive attachment disorder was the wrong diagnosis. Anna displayed selective detachment from her parents.

Because Anna's mother loved horses and dogs, I used this story:

I took in an orphan dog named Copper (not that I intended to compare her daughter to a dog) and put him in the kennel with my other two golden retrievers. When we first took him in, Copper was a great dog. After a couple of weeks, some of the Heartlight kids came over to play with our three dogs. They told me Copper jumped on them, would not listen, constantly barked, acted extremely hyper, and playfully bit one of the girls.

My great idea to take in an orphan dog turned Copper into a bad dog. The problem was not with the dog. The problem was I put him in the kennel. Copper was a young dog that needed to run. He needed more time outside the kennel. He did not need more training. He needed to be given the opportunity to be a dog. I could discipline him all I wanted, but all I really needed to do was change my plan and accommodate his needs.

I complimented Anna's mom for wanting to protect her child from the things of the world. Kids need that. But what Anna needed now without even knowing it was to be given some room to "run," or she would continue to rebel. Too much restriction and control causes anyone to rebel. Anna was responding normally (even though she displayed it inappropriately) to a level of control no longer appropriate for her age.

Randy

When Randy came to live with us, he was sixteen years old. His parents just went through a horrendously nasty divorce. They were consumed with the fight, and did not pay much attention to their son. As a result, Randy started to make his own decisions, do his own thing, and live without any guidance from Mom or Dad.

He tried his best to keep things together and function in two worlds—a home that was falling apart and an everyday life pulling him in new directions. After Randy spent two years pretty much on his own, his mother tried to reengage with him, telling him what to do and placing restrictions on him. Her effort to control challenged his acquired survivor skills. He was used to living without rules, directives, or boundaries.

Randy was resilient and weathered his parents' storm in a way that was amazing for a teenager. However, along the way he failed a few times. Because Mom could not reestablish control, she sent him to live with us.

Randy's sense of humor was attractive and contagious. His people skills were amazing. His compassion for everyone who struggled was touching. He was a salesman at heart (He could sell refrigerators to Eskimos.) who had learned to manipulate his world to survive. These were great skills for someone who lived on his own. Not so great when Mom was trying to get her house in order.

Randy told me he thought the real problem was that he was just too old for his age. He said if he was just two years older, everything he was doing that got him sent to us would be okay. I agreed with him.

Trying to rein in children who already have the control is like using the same old rules with a college kid who returns home after living on his own. It is just never the same. I see this happen quite a bit in various situations: in cases of divorce, when a parent dies and the remaining parent remarries and tries to set up a new home, or when kids are exposed to something or experience something so out of the ordinary they must grow up fast and take control of their lives.

In cases like Randy's, the question is not whether you will hand over control. The question is how to help kids who already have the control function in a home where they do not get to make all the decisions. Randy was not acting like he was too big for his britches. He was too big for his britches.

Todd

Other kids are like Todd, who at sixteen would rather stay isolated at home than go out with friends. (He has none.) He was content with his computer rather than working, going to school, or participating in other social activities. I met Todd's dad following a speaking engagement in Tampa, Fla. He said Todd had no social skills and preferred to watch TV, surf the Internet, play video games, watch movies, or do homework than anything else—all activities that involve no one and require no interaction. Todd's mom said the only control Todd has over his life is the remote control and the keys on his computer.

In elementary school, Todd was allowed to spend inordinate amounts of time on the computer surfing the Internet and playing games. Today, he can find just about any information he wants and can score high on most games. However, Todd did not learn the social skills he needed by his seventh- and eighth-grade years. As a result, those years were socially devastating for him.

Now he isolates himself out of fear, justifiably so. Beneath the fear, Todd has a strong desire to engage with people, but he does not know how to get there. His parents do not know how to get him out of the basement. Todd feels he is so far gone that he gets angry at any attempt to make him interact with people. Todd's parents are so frustrated they would rather leave him alone than rattle his cage.

I talked with Todd about some new boundaries the family decided to adopt. These included limited time in the basement and restricted Internet use. New rules encouraged Todd to get a job, participate in an extracurricular school activity, and eat meals with the family. Todd was given a timeline, direction, and boundaries to stay within. Mom and Dad empowered him by giving him control.

Todd did not like the changes at first. Change is hard—harder than everyone thought it would be. They had a tough road for a while. But as Todd began taking control, a new life unfurled for him. Eventually, he began to enjoy it.

Retaking Control

At times a parent must retake control because a child cannot make good decisions, and some of the bad choices have far-reaching consequences. You must take control when something else has taken control of your child. The way to determine whether you need to retake control is to ask a simple question: If your daughter continues on her present path, where will she be in six months? The answer to that question will determine whether you need to intervene.

Here are some situations that call for a parent's renewed involvement because the consequences could be permanently damaging. The list is not exhaustive. These just happen to be things I see young people wrestle with that demand attention.

First, if you begin to notice your child seems depressed, difficult to motivate, unwilling to participate in life, or suicidal, get him to a therapist or hospital immediately. Even if your child verbally downplays suicide, a teen's action might speak louder than words. No one wants that kind of action.

Second, drinking one time at a party is one thing. Showing up at school or work drunk or getting a DUI is another. Drinking at a party, which about 90 percent of teens do before they graduate from high school, can be corrected with your system of rules and consequences for inappropriate behavior. If your child continues to fail after repeated attempts to curb this behavior, pull in the boundaries a little, increase the consequences, or intervene with outside help.

Showing up at school or work drunk not only indicates a complete disregard for boundaries at home, but also shows a disregard for the rules of society. As a parent, teacher, youth worker, or just someone concerned for the welfare of this child, you must take stronger action now.

The same holds true for drug use. You must take action immediately because of the wide variety and easy access to drugs that are immediately addictive or dangerous, even fatal.

Third, if you find your child is being sexually abused by anyone, you must call the police or the appropriate state agency immediately. The abuser should be removed from the environment immediately. The situation might even require a restraining order. Also, if you believe your child is being exploited or deceived by anyone, whether in person or online, your intervention is necessary. You need to take control.

Fourth, when your children cannot control their habits, patterns, or actions, your intrusion or intercession is necessary, even if they do not want it.

We see more and more teens getting involved with someone much older. When a twenty-four-year-old desires to hang around a sixteen-year-old, something is usually wrong. Formulate rules about social relationships that are appropriate for your child. When healthy boundaries are not in place and someone older becomes possessive or abusive with your child, your involvement is necessary. Running interference is justified.

Your teen's behavior may be a cry for your attention. If your child has one of these problems and you hope it will just go away, you are being irresponsible. These are issues that demand you act quickly.

Giving Up Control

If parents spend less time trying to control their teens and more time helping them develop responsibility and maturity, teens rebel less and act more mature. I watch dads spend years trying to retain control of their kids. They end up losing it anyway. It is inevitable. When they do not transfer control gracefully, they also lose their relationship with their kids. I see moms so fearful their kids might do something wrong they develop an unhealthy attachment. They are unwilling or unable to detach.

In order for children to become healthy adults, they have to become independent from Mom and Dad. Parents can build an environment that will empower their children to blossom in their next stage of life.

CHAPTER THIRTEEN

BUILDING MATURITY BY GIVING RESPONSIBILITY

*W*ouldn't you love to see your teen display mature and responsible behavior? Make good decisions? Use good judgment? Stand on good principles? Exhibit integrity? I wrestled for years to come up with a formula to motivate immature kids to start thinking with good sense and wisdom.

I concluded that maturity follows responsibility. This clarifies parents' immediate goal: to encourage their children to accept responsibility. How do they do that? By releasing control of their children's possible failures and by helping their children understand that the acceptance of responsibility develops the maturity they desire.

I am amazed how many parents want their teens to be mature, yet the parents retain a level of control that prevents their kids from taking any responsibility. Most parents probably do not keep all the control intentionally. They keep it because they desire to be involved in their kids' lives, but they do so by commands and a zealous desire to ensure their children do not mess up.

David Damico implies in his book *The Faces of Rage* that parents' mistakes in raising kids are not usually parental error as much as parental ignorance.[1] So true. Most mistakes are not intentional; they are the result of not knowing any better, of trying to solve one problem and unintentionally creating another.

In order for teens to be responsible, they have to be given something to be responsible for. They have to be given control. They have to be allowed to make decisions and choices. They must be able to exercise and practice their judgment. They do these within the boundaries you set for their journey through the teen years. And they must be allowed to fail.

Oscar Wilde insightfully tells us, "Experience is the name everyone gives to their mistakes."[2] If you want your relationship with your children to go deeper than ever, stick with them when they fail or struggle to fulfill their obligations (a good sign of responsibility). Let your words become flesh, and be there to demonstrate your love for them, not to control but to guide.

James Belasco and Ralph Stayer state in their book *Flight of the Buffalo*, "Most of us overestimate the value of what we currently have, and have to give up, and underestimate the value of what we might gain."[3] That is beautifully put.

Andy Law of the Creative Company stated, "Unless you are pre-pared to give up something valuable you will never be able to truly change at all, because you will be forever in the control of things you can't give up."[4]

If you are to help your children grow up, you must grow up as well. Help them grow, let them grow, and grow with them. To show them how to make a healthy life, you have to have a healthy life. To encourage them to make wise choices, you have to make wise choices. To require that they act responsibly, you have to be re-sponsible. Demanding them to be mature means you need to be mature. To demonstrate the need for change, you must be willing to share with them the changes in your life. That's a life-on-life experience that sharpens one another. Both lives are better for it.

When you create an atmosphere of change in relationship with your children, you plant within their hearts a hope that lets them see a future full of possibilities. Give it to them!

Rebecca

Rebecca's mom wanted to make up for all the ways she failed her daughter. She gave birth to Rebecca at fifteen, believed she allowed Rebecca's father to die, and never became the mother she wanted to be. Rebecca's mom determined to make up for all her mistakes by controlling her daughter's life and making everything right.

Rebecca grew more and more immature as the days passed. At fourteen, Rebecca was motivated to work towards independence and responsibility. Now eighteen, she was reduced to an emotionally crippled young woman who would rather stay at Heartlight than go home. She cut herself to express her frustration over her mother's sovereignty cloaked in acts of service.

Mom did not have a clue. She may not still. She cannot comprehend how her daughter could end up in the place she is. Mom tearfully commented, "I did everything for her." And she did. That was exactly the problem. Rebecca's attempts to share her with her mother fell on deaf ears. The relationship began to show the strain of her mom's total control, and Rebecca moved on to where she could take control of her life, grab responsibility by the horns, and live the life God intended. In this case, cutting the emotional umbilical cord to Mom was a wrenching but necessary move.

It was harder on Mom. She calls regularly asking what she can do to get her daughter back. There is nothing she can do. She did not give her daughter responsibility for her own life at the appropriate time. Now Rebecca steers clear so as not to fall prey to codependence again. As Rebecca matures and creates her own family, perhaps the relationship will be healed and restored. I am hopeful that, in time, Rebecca will figure out how to erect healthy boundaries with her mother, since her mother was unable to get to that point with her. The sad part is Rebecca's mom lost her by trying to give her daughter something she never had. She wanted to prove her worthiness as a mother, but only ended up emotionally smothering her daughter.

Some of the most mature and wise adults I know are those who went through horrendous times during their adolescent years.

Crime, divorce, death of parents, and abandonment created environments where they had to accept responsibility for their lives in order to survive. Kids never cease to amaze me in their resiliency and ability to adapt to horrific situations or circumstances that require them to take on responsibility prematurely. Just about every kid I know who experienced this level of adversity has stepped up to the plate, swung well, and hit a few homers. They may also ground out, hit a pop fly, or get thrown out at the plate a few times; but they choose to stay in the game and stick to their positions. Though they were forced to mature sooner than their peers, these young people do well. Your child is capable of the same.

I encourage parents to give their children treasured possessions now instead of waiting to leave an inheritance. You are going to give them anyway, so why not give while the act of giving can strengthen the relationship and demonstrate how much you value your children—even when they do not deserve it? Must a child always do well to receive parents' grace? Grace would not be called grace if that was true, would it?

Giving It to Them

Believe it or not, most teens develop maturity from the outside in. We clothe them in maturity, trusting it will be internalized. For teens, the one thing worse than not getting what they want is getting what they want too easily. Teens want control; they just fear the responsibility that comes with it. Responsibility must be handed to them so they can practice decision-making and control over their lives before they leave your home and try to make it on their own.

I talked with a lady in the Toledo airport who asked me if I knew what the greatest gift parents could give their children might be. As I thought, she interjected, "Make them get a job. It will teach them lessons about responsibility they should have learned at home."

Sadly, she may be correct. Today, I see many homes where responsibility is never developed. Issues of control are not defined the way they should be. In the workplace, workers know their jobs and accept that managers have authority. Correction is not an issue. Employees know who writes the paycheck. Those who do not respect the manager or follow the rules get fired. End of story. Do your kids know what and who they are working for in your home? Do they know why you are transferring things to them and requiring things of them?

You must empower them to make decisions. Tell them they have the freedom to choose from the options you offer. Communicate your intentions with phrases like, "You choose," "That's your choice," "It's up to you," "I'll support you in whatever you decide," "Hey, you're the man—you make the call," and "Sweetheart, this is something you're going to have to decide." Give them the chance to exercise good judgment while you can still observe, guide, and gently correct.

When you empower your children this way, you affirm them. You also allow for the possibility they might make the wrong decision. Sometimes that is okay. Let them fail, even when you make things right by intervening. For instance, you could force your fourteen-year-old son to finish mowing the yard before dark by reminding him repeatedly. However, the greater lesson is that by not getting it finished before dark, he may not go out with his friends that night. The sting of the consequence carries greater weight than your constant nagging to get things done.

When your eighteen-year-old daughter does not apply to college, you could force her to fill out all the applications. You could do it for her. However, maybe the best thing is to tell her once, place the papers in her room, and leave her alone. If she fills them out and gets accepted, your relationship is less tense because you did not nag. She also proved to you and herself she could get it done. On the other hand, she may not do them and may lose her chance of getting accepted. If she is not motivated to apply, what makes you think she will be motivated to succeed if you do it for her?

She needs to learn to take responsibility for what she wants to do in life. She needs to experience the reality that adults will not do her work for her. She also learns to complete a task, respect schools' requirements, and expect consequences—good or bad—according to her choices. Learning comes best when your child is given responsibility and has no recourse or escape from the results of her actions or lack of action.

Give your children the freedom to make decisions about academics. I tell young people all the time whether or not they graduate from high school is up to them. You might help them any way you can. You may support them any way they ask. But you cannot be responsible for their academics. Academics are their responsibility.

When your child goes off to college, keep boundaries in place during these years. If your child is immature, consider a small Christian school with more boundaries than a larger state school. Tell him you will pay for him to go to school at one of four particular colleges (your boundary), and he gets to choose which one he goes to (his responsibility).

When your child decides to get a job during school, let him choose his work hours so he has to learn juggle his work schedule, class load, and social life. Your son needs to figure out how to balance his schedule and budget his money. Your daughter should handle her own issues at work. Life requires good balance between the demands at home and demands at work. Your kids need to know how to negotiate with a boss and how to be part of a family. These same issues pop up in marriage, right? Couples with kids struggle to find balance, so learning balance in the high school and college years gives them a head start in creating healthy solutions and compromises when they have a family of their own. Maintaining relationships is vital during the difficult teen years. So is training your child to be successful.

You are not disengaging when you tell them they must be responsible for some of their own decisions. Furthermore, as long as the "money highway" flows between you and your children, you have the right to give the money with strings attached. They need to choose whether they continue to get funding from you. They should submit to the conditions of the family rules and maintain their own responsibilities before you pay for their activities, possessions, and lifestyle.

I encourage families to give their children a checkbook in the eighth grade. Figure out how much you spend on each child in a month for school supplies, lunches, allowance, clothes, and special-event money. Open bank accounts. Let them know the funds you deposit must cover all their expenses for the month. Your children might just surprise you. Your daughter will either do very well and balance her funds or come home from the mall with a two-hundred-dollar pair of jeans and eat a lot of tuna fish or peanut butter all month.

This is where learning takes place if you do not bail her out by giving her more money. If you do, she will never realize where she failed and will have to learn another way. If your son needs lunch money before the end of the month, suggest he take the items he blew his funds on and sell them. Or give him a bigger workload around the house and let him earn more money on a one-time basis. Challenge him to get creative (without doing anything immoral, illicit, or illegal) to get more money. Maybe your daughter will sell those new jeans on eBay or Craigslist for a profit. Kids' ingenuity never ceases to amaze me.

When you make your kids solve their own problems, you give them responsibility. You help them learn decision-making. If and when they fail, let them feel the consequences. I have yet to hear of a teen starving to death while wearing that two-hundred-dollar pair of jeans. These training opportunities might save their finances, marriage, or relationship with their own kids one day. This is how a teen gathers wisdom.

Give kids the responsibility to do their own laundry. Let them cook meals for the family. Give them more opportunities than you think they can handle. Let them try. Let them feel what it is like to live in a world where they need to set boundaries. Kids are resilient. They want to make decisions. They want to be in control. Hand it over now while course correction is easy. Later, the consequences are steeper and the price a lot higher to pay.

Jim

Jim's mother always answered his questions. He never had to think for himself. Jim did not have to think through anything. His mom was smart and capable, and she often figured out the answers for everyone around her. She was amazing. If she heard a question, she answered it even if it was not asked of her!

As a result, seventeen-year-old Jim did not know how to figure anything out—answers, solutions, remedies to situations, wisdom, or steps to take toward his future. His mother's incessant answers to every question, combined with her justification of Jim's inappropriate behavior, were astounding. Jim is a nice young man, but he is frightened by the thought of living on his own. He should be. He is not prepared to live without Mom.

I encouraged his mother over a period of months to let Jim seek his own answers. Unfortunately, Jim shut down by then and was not motivated to ask questions. When he stopped, Mom stepped in further and began telling Jim the questions he should be asking. Then she answered them—all in the same breath.

When teens ask questions, parents can easily give answers and steer the conversation in the right direction. But easy answers and declarations stifle relationships. When kids want to talk, the last thing they need is a lecture. They just need a good listener while they puzzle it out.

Answering all your child's questions precludes wonderment and creativity, takes away the challenge of figuring anything out, and stops the search for learning. Think about the value of putting a puzzle together, hunting for Easter eggs, seeking information for a research project, or doing a crossword puzzle. The fun and excitement of these is in the search, not the end result. I take Mensa intelligence tests in airline magazines just to make sure I still have the ability to think. (It's questionable at times.) If I cheat by jumping to the answers listed on the next page, the challenge and the fun are immediately over. Providing answers to your teens' questions will stop some very good and necessary logical and sequential thinking. The journey is usually more valuable than the destination.

To find out how much you answer your teen's questions, spend the weekend not saying a word unless you are spoken to. Strive only to answer questions with questions. Do not give your opinion for a whole weekend. This little exercise will show you how much your teen hangs onto your answers and thinking. If you want your child to be an independent thinker and to use his head as you give him more responsibility, you must wean him from an unhealthy dependency on you and your brain.

One way to help train kids to assume responsibility is to stop reminding them of appointments. Post them on the refrigerator calendar, or meet with them periodically to put them in their phone or planner. They are capable of looking at the calendar from there. Quit waking them up for school. They are old enough to set an alarm and get out of bed by themselves. Most young people want to graduate from high school and will do what is necessary to make that happen. Your child may oversleep on occasion as he gets used to waking up on his own, but he will learn. Likewise, you are not responsible for his job. He is. You are not responsible to do his laundry or clean his room. He is.

I hope you understand I am *not* saying stop spending time with your kids, ignore their needs, and fail to engage with them when you are invited into their space. Remain engaged in every way. Just gradually hand over the jobs you do for your kids. If you transfer the tasks and responsibilities to them, you lead them to maturity.

What If They Won't Take It?

Transferring responsibility to your child is especially important if you are dealing with a child who is struggling. This is an awkward and confusing situation because parents are reluctant to let kids assume responsibility when they do not trust them. Kids are already acting irresponsibly. Why would you trust them with more? It is further complicated when parents have to take control because the kids are spinning out of control.

In the short term, parents have to do what they have to do when their kids' behavior has potential far-reaching and life-threatening consequences. But parents' short-term control should lead to the long-term goal of giving kids responsibility for their own lives.

Continue to focus on your belief system, your authority in the house as a parent, and your desire to see your child grow and understand the importance of consequences.

Let me give you an example. Let's say your child comes home drunk again. You might find a time to say something like this:

> Sarah, we need to discuss some things you and I know are not in line with what we all agreed about the use of alcohol. This has happened before, so you are forcing me to take your car away. I want you to drive, but we had an agreement. What I have been doing does not seem to be working, and I can't just sit back and do nothing. I cannot allow the daughter I love to take a path that will destroy her. I am not going to let that happen. That would not be loving you. We are going to see a counselor, and until he or she gives me a "thumbs up" that you can commit to quit drinking, you are going to be grounded.
>
> I need the keys to the car. I applaud you for getting someone else to drive, but your continual reckless behavior is causing me to have to act. You get the car back when I know you have gone six weekends without drinking after you are no longer grounded.

Understand I am not going to sit back and watch you continually exercise bad judgment. If you continue to do what you're doing, you're going to end up in a place you don't want to be. I am going to work my hardest to make sure that doesn't happen. I am fighting for you, Sarah, and I won't stop because I love you too much to let you destroy your life.

A statement like this is an affirmation of your relationship with your daughter. It has some bite to it. It applies consequences. It holds firm and upholds family values and beliefs. It tells Sarah, "This is not about me; it's about you, Sweetheart." It also gives Sarah hope that losing the car and grounding are not forever. It offers help (counseling) and an action plan for Sarah to get her freedom and driving privileges back. This is important because if the consequences seem endless or too harsh, teens will give up and do nothing. If there is nothing they can do to be restored, they might as well stew in their own juices, so to speak.

Be ready for your child to try to shift the blame.

"Dad, all I had was one drink. Someone must have put more alcohol in the punch."

"Dad, that cop would never have known I was drunk if you fixed the taillight on the car."

"It's not my fault they have these stupid laws."

"Well, if Sharon brought me home when she said she would, I wouldn't have been drunk and you would have never known."

Here is your response: "This is your deal, Sweetheart. You are responsible for yourself. I really don't care about what anyone else did or did not do. This is about you, your life, and what is required of you."

Or she may try to justify it all:

"Dad, everyone in my class drinks. You and Mom make these rules that are so stupid."

"Sally's parents let her drink, and she's sixteen, so I thought it would be okay."

"It was Sean's birthday, and we just celebrated."

"It was just this one time, Dad."

"I waited to drive home, Dad."

"I am almost an adult, Dad. Didn't you drink when you were eighteen?"

"I am going to drink, and you're not going to stop me."

Or she may try to give the following excuses:

"I couldn't quit."

"I felt pressured."

"I didn't know alcohol was in there."

"I thought it was Pepsi and didn't know there was vodka in the drink."

"Jason gave it to me and didn't tell me."

"There's nothing wrong with what I did, so if you and Mom want to carry out your little rules, fine."

"Whatever!"

Or she may try to minimize what just happened:

"Come on, Dad, it's not that big of a deal."

"You and Mom are trying to make this bigger than it is."

"I don't need a counselor! It's not like I have a drinking problem or something."

"Just four beers, Dad; it's not like I was really drunk or something."

Whatever she says, your message remains the same. Focus on the bigger picture when caught in this barrage of blame shifting, justification, excuses, or minimizing the bad behavior. Remember, the bigger picture is not about drinking; it's about responsibility. This would be my response to Sarah:

It's not about being drunk; it's about respect for what we all agreed to. It's not about someone else. It's about you. This is your deal. It's no one else's fault. It is a problem because it continues to happen. No excuse will move me to say what you did was okay. You and I agreed we did not want to be on this path, and I am not giving up my part of the agreement because you want to back out of yours. You chose to lose the car because that is the family rule. You chose to be grounded because that's what we agreed to. You choose your own consequences. You are making some irresponsible choices that you can't pin on anyone other than yourself, Sarah. I am sorry you put yourself in this position.

Can you hear the real message behind these words? "I want you to be responsible. Because you are involved in something that could eventually control you or hurt you, we are going to bump up the consequences a little."

Remember the presenting behavior is usually not the underlying problem, so the next conversation may be spent dealing with the heart of the matter. Two separate things are happening, and you need to be careful not to confuse them. When a child comes home drunk, it may not be the time to talk about the underlying issues.

When the time is right to talk about the underlying issues, do not ask, "How many drinks did you have at that party on May third at one a.m. when you were with Sean and Sally?" Keep the issue separate from the behavior, and deal with each of them differently. Stay strong on the consequences for behavior and the assumption of responsibility and soft on the motivating factors for the behavior.

Maturity

Maturity is a character trait that combines experience, wisdom, knowledge, a solid foundation, good decision-making, and common sense. Maturity happens as a result of being responsible. It is something we all want to see in our kids. It assures parents they have done well in their child-rearing. It is a character trait that will be carried throughout the rest of a child's life. But it only happens when parents create an environment that encourages and sometimes demands responsibility from their children. Start today!

CHAPTER FOURTEEN

WE'RE SPINNING OUT OF CONTROL

One of parents' worst nightmares is to see their families spinning out of control, to be unable to stop the rapid descent into a full-fledged crash.

If you are currently experiencing that feeling of helplessness, hopelessness, and fear, I strongly encourage you to take action quickly. Talk to someone—a friend, pastor, youth minister, counselor, your own parent, or mentor. I urge you to gain outside wisdom regarding your situation. Ask for help. Stop at nothing until you find an answer. The course you take when your child is acting wild and unrestrained might determine whether your future will include your child in it.

Choosing to Intervene

Three stages take you to the point of intervention where you involve someone else in your family's business. The first stage is accepting what is actually happening within your family. The second stage is justifying the intervention. The third stage is plotting a course and pulling your child out of his or her nosedive.

Accepting the reality of the problem is difficult for some parents. Many just can't acknowledge or recognize the severity of the problem. Parents who see only the good, hope for the best, and believe no wrong are usually blind to what everyone around them already sees. Admittedly, because problems often develop gradually, it is easy for them to miss the signs. Friends, neighbors, and those around the family may see what is happening, but they may not know how to convince the parents of something the parents do not see. If you wonder if you have blinders on, ask those closest to you. Seek wise counsel and receive their observations without becoming defensive. They probably know what's going on.

That forms the foundation of the second stage: justifying the intervention. Other people should agree with your decision to intervene in some way, encouraging you to do something. You will need this support as you take the next step.

The third stage is a little lonelier, especially if you have to remove your child from the home. Most parents I meet mention that when the decision came down to removing their child from the home, they felt quite isolated and sometimes even excommunicated. Taking action can be painful, and most people avoid pain. Friends will describe your situation to others as a sad time, a painful time, and a time they hope they do not have to go through with their children. Their description will hurt, but it is true. You would not wish your situation on any of your friends or loved ones, would you?

Teens spin out of control when they do not have the internal ability to function externally within the established boundaries and rules of a home.

The resulting behaviors, if allowed to continue, could have dangerous or grave consequences.

Intervention is necessary to protect the child and deal with the issues that led to the behavior. I am sure plenty of conversations with your child about your concerns took place before you got to this point. You tried and tried to get through and correct their course with little success. Perhaps you even implemented boundaries and helped your child understand consequences. If you did not, I suggest you start quickly.

But at some point, when all else fails, you are the one who needs to make decisions about the next step. What your child thinks is somewhat immaterial by now, as he or she is obviously not thinking clearly or maturely.

This is not the time to mull over where everything went wrong. It is not a time to shift the blame, make accusations, question motives, or withdraw and disengage from your child. It is the time for action. It is not the time to focus on whether you are a failure as a parent. It is the time to make sure you do not fail to help now when your teen needs you the most.

Do We Need Help?

Often parents struggle to determine if their children need help. Has your child's behavior deteriorated in the last six months? Do you have reason to believe it will continue to worsen in the next six months?

Your first line of offense with your out-of-control teen is to utilize the resources around you. Perhaps this will ward off any further difficulty and pull your child out of the nosedive. That first line might include your child's teachers, the school administration, a Sunday school teacher, other parents of kids at church, your pastor, your parents, your siblings, your friends, your Bible study group, a counseling hotline, the older couple down the street, a youth minister, a Young Life leader, or just about anyone who has contact with your child. Even his or her friends. In fact, if your teen's friends show up at your home, ask them what's going on. Some will not be afraid to answer; they might be concerned as well. Make sure you ask questions, and let people know it is okay to be honest with you.

Voltaire once said, "Common sense is not so common." An old Chinese proverb says, "He who asks is a fool for five minutes, but he who does not ask remains a fool forever." Proverbs 15:22 (NIV) agrees: "Plans fail for lack of counsel, but with many advisers they succeed."

After you get counsel and spend time thinking it through, start to put your plan into action. Perhaps your child needs to go to counseling. If so, put that requirement into your rules or belief system at home. If the counselor determines your child needs some type of medication, trust what the counselor says. See a psychiatrist who understands teens and their issues. Try the medication.

Surround yourself with people you trust, so when you ask for their counsel and they tell you what you do not want to hear, you trust them. If you pick and choose the counsel you receive, you will more than likely continue to do what you want, and your child will continue to spin out of control.

One personal recommendation: Do not let old beliefs about medicine control your new decisions. If your child is depressed, diagnosed with attention deficit disorder, hyperactive, unable to sleep at night, bipolar, overly anxious, or has a mental condition that would respond to medication, do not let any outdated notions keep you from getting your child help.

Hospitalization is needed whenever children might harm themselves. Extreme cutting, depression, eating disorders, suicidal thoughts, or excessive drug or alcohol use are just a few of the symptoms that might warrant hospitalization. If you know there is a big problem, but you do not know exactly what it is, trust your gut. Do not hesitate to hospitalize your child if you fear for his life or safety. It is better to be safe than sorry.

Residential Programs

If all your efforts are fruitless and your child is not responding to any at-home interventions, consider placing your teen in an alternative residential setting. No doubt this will be one of the hardest decisions you ever have to make. Having a child leave home is not an easy decision, nor is it a small task. However, once you make the decision, you can begin the search for the right placement.

You have many options to consider. I am quite biased toward our residential program, Heartlight, in Hallsville, Texas, but other programs offer different formats that might fit your needs better. A wilderness camp works well for rebellious kids who need activity and physical challenges to get their attention. They are usually thirty- to sixty-day programs that remove kids from their familiar environments and allow them to spend time talking, reflecting, and confronting their issues. The new environment is controlled by natural boundaries. Those who participate in wilderness programs usually need some type of follow-up residential or outpatient program. The two programs complement each other and, in the long run, end up saving time and money.

As I mentioned above, hospitalization is needed when kids endanger themselves, self-injure, or have severe alcohol or drug problems. They need to detoxify and get medical intervention. This stay is usually a temporary "hold" until you can find a long-term program.

Therapeutic boarding schools include counseling or small-group therapy. They also address therapeutic and educational needs of each resident. Heartlight would be classified as a therapeutic boarding school.

Some programs operate overseas. Explore any program like this carefully, paying special attention to the staff of the program. Make sure you meet those who will be supervising your child. Moving a problem child to another country with minimum compliance standards is not always the answer to your teen's needs. This may prevent your involvement with your child and fail to give your child the adequate help he or she needs.

To find out more information about options, explore the Internet and review the materials for each program. Seek out other families who placed their child away from home for a season. Ask difficult questions and make sure you visit the campus before taking your child anywhere.

How Did They Know?

Parents realize the need to take action in different ways. The progression is usually the same. They come to the stark reality their situation with their teen is out of control, their attempts to correct are not working, and their predicament demands immediate attention.

A while back I asked families that were currently with us at Heartlight to complete this sentence: I knew my child was spinning out of control when _____.

Here are some of their responses:

> "Our entire family was being controlled by her behavior. My marriage was failing; my relationship with my older daughter was suffering. I was not eating, sleeping, or

performing well at work. I was beginning to withdraw from social settings and felt like my family was falling apart. Every option I tried failed."

"She stopped smiling and refused to get up and go to school."

"Everything got crazy. The cell phone bill listed phone calls in the middle of the night, and her only response was, 'So what?' She started running away and said her two-year-old sister unlocked all the downstairs windows so she could sneak back in late at night. The new shoes I bought for an anniversary cruise suddenly went missing after she told me how 'hot' they were and how all her friends wanted them. I can go on and on … the list never ends. We felt helpless."

"Her attitude changed. She was more argumentative and defiant. She began hanging out with a different group of kids, who I later found out were experimenting with drugs and alcohol."

"He became as physical as he was verbal!"

"He began hanging out with a pretty rough crew. That's when his attitude toward us as parents made a complete change overnight, and he began to hate everything we said or did."

"She began cutting and became obsessed with killing herself in order to go to Heaven to be with her dad. I was afraid to leave her alone. She was a sad little girl. She was meeting with a therapist, her youth minister, her Sunday school teacher, and her school counselor. They were all taking extra time with her and pouring their lives into her. All of these interventions were not effective. One night she came right out and said, 'I need more help. I have no more desire to live or stop cutting than I did before everyone started helping me. I just want to die; I don't like feeling this way.'"

"I realized I had exhausted all of the parental tools I had to control the direction of her life."

"She couldn't get over her dad's death. Her depression was controlling her. She wanted help more than I wanted it for her and begged me to find her a place where she could get it."

"She looked me in the eye and said, 'I am going to do whatever I want and there is not a thing you can do about it!'"

"He was arrested three times in three months for possession of marijuana, and he chose to go to juvenile detention center rather than come home and be under house arrest. He violated the plan we set in place, and he knew if he defied me again, he had to leave. The situation was tough, but the decision was easy. He made it for me."

"Our son was not responding to our efforts to help him. He ran away from home for the second time and was brought home by the local police. Our efforts at changing schools and participating in family counseling with him for the previous four months were not helping, and our counselor recommended we find a different place for him to live."

"She started cutting herself and continued to skip school even in the face of probation."

"I looked into his big, brown eyes and saw that the spark he always had was gone. All I saw was a look of hopelessness and darkness, a silent cry for help. I knew it was time to find something or someone to help bring that spark of light and hope back into my son's eyes."

"He became disrespectful to his parents, sisters, teachers, and stepparents. He was abusive, verbally and possibly physically, to his girlfriends. He left school when he wanted and got suspended."

"My son looked at my wife and said, 'If you don't shut your mouth, I'll shut if for you.'"

"We were calling the police several times a week, not knowing if or when she was coming home. We never knew who she was with or where she was. The police told us to do something now or things will only get worse."

"My daughter came into my bedroom crying late one night and said, 'Mom and Dad, I need help.'"

"Our son ignored everything we said, did everything we did not want him to do, and said nasty things we never thought would come out of his mouth."

When It's Time

The following checklist includes some behaviors that reveal the possible need to place your child outside your home:

- When your teen will not listen to reason and is becoming increasingly disrespectful, dishonest, and disobedient, openly displaying his rebellious actions.

- When there is physical contact or threats.

- When a bad habit or addiction has engulfed your child.

- When your child is displaying behavior that is a marked change from what used to be normal (sleeping longer, being forgetful, losing motivation, being depression, hating what she once loved, and loving what she once hated).

- When your child blatantly ignores or profoundly rebels against your boundaries, belief system, or rules of the home. This can be shown in passive-aggressive or openly defiant behavior.

- When your teen is too depressed to function within normal expectations at home.

- When your child displays no conscience about his actions, the consequences, or the effects of his behavior on himself or other family members.

- When suicidal thoughts and comments arise.

- When your child treats people, pets, or belongings, in a threatening or overly unruly way.

- When your child's behavior puts him or her in danger or at high risk.

- When post-traumatic behaviors of drinking, taking drugs, or being sexually active are present.

- When your teen's continued disregard for others in the family causes ongoing strife, sleepless nights, and trauma to other siblings, and you can't stop it.

This checklist is not exhaustive, but these seem to be the common reasons parents place children outside their home.

Chris

When people are in pain, they do pretty weird things. The first time I picked up a child to come live in our residential program, I flew to Nashville. I met Chris's father at the airport, and he told me his son was at a local park. That was where we were going to pick him up. Chris's dad and I expected Chris to cry a little, yell and scream, and then reluctantly come with me.

That was our expectation, but it did not quite work that way. The minute Chris and I were introduced and his dad said, "Mark is going to take you back to Texas with him," I caught a right jab to my right eye and cheekbone that knocked me to the ground. It was the only time I ever saw stars during daylight! I ended up with a big black eye. As I was coming to, I rolled over to watch Chris running through the woods to get away from me, and I heard his dad say, "I guess we should have done something different." *Imagine that*, I thought to myself.

As we walked back to the car to discuss Plan B, I caught myself asking God, *You called me to this? Are you sure?* But I learned a great lesson. I have never been hit again.

The lesson was this: Be prepared. People in pain do some pretty weird things. To make a long story short, I got back on the plane that night alone. Two days later, my eye was still black, and my cheek was still swollen, but Chris moved into the guys' house. He apologized, and we got along fine for years. Whenever I think of Chris, I wink my eye. He does not remember what happened. He was higher than a kite that day. Whenever I hear someone say, "I guess we should have done something different," I think of Chris's dad. Be prepared for anything when you encounter a teen out of control.

Phil

I learned a second lesson about confronting kids with Phil. Phil's parents asked me to pick him up at their home, and they assured me he would be there. They did not tell me he ran away a few days earlier. They feared I would not come if they did not know where he was. When I arrived at their home, they told me he was at a KISS concert and he would be easy to find because they knew where he was sitting and because he had red hair. Sounded good to me.

I sat in the parking lot, strategizing the best way to get Phil to come with me. In my immature brilliance, I decided to tell him his parents were in an accident, and I was sent to pick him up and take him home. As I walked into the concert, I could not hear myself think because the music was so loud. It was dark, and all I had was a picture of the young man. After an hour of squinting, I finally found him. I walked up to him and noticed he was drunk. I thought his condition would work in my favor because he would not be thinking too well. It worked. He walked out with me. As we started to drive, I shared with him we were actually headed to a program where we could help him.

Because I lied to him, he never trusted me. Phil never connected with me or anyone at Heartlight. I blame it squarely on the way I brought him there. The lesson? Do not lie when you are in a difficult situation with your child. It will come back and bite you at a later date.

Will

Will taught me a third lesson. I drove to Little Rock, Ark., with a fellow who knew a family dealing with a son messed up on drugs again. We were going to pick him up and take him back home with us. When we confronted Will, he ran, cussing at the top of his lungs. He slipped on a dishrag on the floor and hit his head against the cabinets. While we were sitting at the hospital waiting for him to get stitched up, I asked again, *Lord, are you positive you called me to this?* (I asked myself that a lot in the early days of working with kids.)

Will got in the backseat of the car, and we drove the few hours home. I thought I botched everything. But in the back of my 1982 white Ford Bronco, Will accepted Christ. On his own. He calls the scar on his cheek his "Jesus scar." This third lesson: Stand firm. Even though someone runs, something goes bad, or someone cusses at you, God can bring that person to a relationship with Him. I think of Will whenever I see a white Bronco.

Be Prepared. Don't Lie. Stand Firm. Good wisdom for those preparing to do battle for the lives of their children. Love is sometimes tough. Your efforts to save the life of your child will never be forgotten.

CHAPTER FIFTEEN

HOPE IN DIFFICULT TIMES

I grew up in a generation bent on finding peace. Did you? The peace emblem was on every black-light poster and tie-dyed shirt I had. It was the "Give peace a chance" generation, filled with peace movements and rallies. Peace was promoted in relationships, flashed with our V-signs, and yelled from the rooftops in our pursuit of world harmony.

I watched a television commercial the other day that stated, "We put the meaning in meaningful relationships." We did. While we "peaced" everything together, we threw out something pretty important—the concept of allowing relationships to survive conflict. We were so set on finding oneness we ran from anything that hinted of conflict, struggle, and hardship. In doing so, my generation ran from marriages, denied anything negative happened to our children, and created a generation gap of a different sort than we experienced as adolescents.

That absence of struggle continues today, as parents want their children to have it easier and better than they had. But easier keeps relationships from moving to the depth we really long for. The relationship pendulum has moved too far to one side, pointing to peace at all costs.

Divorce rates are higher than they have been the last twenty-five years. Sadly, many of the family struggles today are the result of my generation's well-intentioned pursuit to "put the meaning into meaningful relationships." Because our parents were often hard-working but distant, we tried so hard to connect that we unintentionally caused heartache and hurt as people disappear during difficult times.

It is no wonder children fear abandonment if there is conflict. That is what they see growing up today. When the going gets tough, the peace-lovers get going, ill-equipped to push through conflict to achieve resolution.

Is there hope? Yes, there is. Hope for a kind of true peace that allows the conflict and struggle in our lives to lead us to stronger and deeper relationships with those we love.

The world's view of peace is the absence of conflict. God's definition of peace is hope in the midst of conflict.

On the other side of this current crisis or impending hardship with your teen, you will be fine. You may even be better if you deal with issues head-on, rather than ignoring them or walking away.

I recently met a family who lost their son the night before. I told them how sorry I was they had to go through something like this. I shared my shock, grief, and hurt, all the time assuring them God would get them through this difficult time.

The boy's dad looked at me and said, "I don't think I can do this." Tears streamed down his face.

I could barely get the words past the flood of emotion I felt as I cried with him. "Ben," I said, "if I had told you yesterday your son was going to die tonight …"

He interrupted me with the words, "I think I would have told you I could not handle that." He paused for me to continue.

"That's the point," I said. "You didn't think you could, but you did. You are. You will make it to the other side of this tragedy. God will walk you through it and be with you the whole way. I promise."

I have led Young Life groups in which kids have died, and sat with lost and grieving families experiencing excruciating pain. It tears me up every time. Even now, my eyes well thinking about the losses families I know experienced. I have buried kids I loved, kids I spent many good times with—all victims of malice, accidents, or cancer. I have sat for hours with parents who felt as if they could not go on, could not even breathe. But they did.

The thousands of kids we lived with through the years struggled immensely. My wife and I shed plenty of tears with their parents. At the time, these moms and dads could not see any light at the end of their families' dark tunnels. But they made it through.

I lead thousands of counseling sessions, phone conversations, and conference calls with moms and dads who are worn out. They are tired of being called every name in the book, challenged on every level and belief they ever held, and absolutely depleted because of all the hardships caused by their teen. All of them believe they are not going to survive what is in front of them. But they do.

I have given just about every weekend of my adult life to families across this country, speaking at seminars to parents caught in family crises, parents feeling as if their worlds are falling apart. Many lost hope and did not think they were going to make it. But they did.

I talk to people in radio interviews, in airports, at churches, when I am out to eat, and wherever I speak. So many are desperate, looking for answers to all the questions their teens' behaviors pose. Many think they will never get past this traumatic experience of their teen spinning out of control, but they do. They will.

You will too.

My college degree is in finance with an emphasis on investments. I know this:

There is no greater investment you can make than investing in the life of your child.

Even when the market is down and you are not seeing the return you hoped for, do not bail. Stick it out.

Your child is a unique masterpiece, covered with the fingerprints of our heavenly Father, who knew where to place His treasure. Of all the people He created in this world, He entrusted this particular child to you. You have one-of-a-kind gifts and talents to share with this young individual in your life. The time you give and the effort you invest will one day pay off. And the payoff will be great.

By investing in your teen, you also sow into your teen's future marriage, your future daughter- or son-in-law, your future grandchildren, and into the life God gave you. So don't give up. Keep your interest high and make your investment one of longevity.

Remember the verse in Galatians I shared back in Chapter Two? The one where Paul reminds us of our return? It's Galatians 6:9, and let's read it one more time. Post it on your refrigerator. Stick it on your bathroom mirror. Tape it to your steering wheel. Repeat it to yourself with gritted teeth the next time your teen gets in your face and tempts you to walk away for good.

"Let us not become weary in doing good, for at the proper time we will reap a harvest **if we do not give up**" (NIV, emphasis mine).

What Does Hope Look Like?

I heard a story years ago about Abraham Lincoln leaving a church service on a Sunday afternoon. It was raining horrendously and had evidently been raining for quite some time. As he and a colleague were surveying the downpour, the colleague asked, "Think it will ever quit?" President Lincoln's two-word answer helps me through tough times, whether mine or those around me. He profoundly answered, "Always does."

Somehow, just knowing whatever pain I feel will pass helps me endure the pain I experience. Tell me it will be over. Tell me the dentist drilling on my tooth will finish soon. Assure me the grief I feel will leave. Just promise me this momentary affliction will be over one day. Swear to me the hurt and pain I feel will quit.

Always does.

When I meet with families in dire need of help with their teens, I lay an important foundational perspective: I am more concerned with where their teens will be five years from now than I am in getting them through the current conflict. The inappropriate behavior of their children may have finally forced these parents to sit across from me to try and figure out a solution, but that is not the focus of our conversation.

Sure, the inappropriate behavior must stop, but the real question for me is, "What must you do today to ensure your child has a great relationship with you five years from now?" In most cases, families manage to get through the difficult days, and the troubled teen and parents end up having a great relationship in the future.

Why Try?

Parents often ask me, "If my child is going to get through the issues anyway, and we are all going to be fine, then why even work on dealing with the issues?" That's a good question that deserves an answer. Here's an analogy:

A man is rushed to the hospital after suffering a stroke. He gets to the emergency room and the doctor looks at him and says, "I think there is hope for a good outcome with your condition—if you use the medication we have available."

His family is incredibly encouraged and full of hope. But no one does anything. They do not fill the prescription The man does not use the medication. The man's condition deteriorates, and the family begins to lose hope.

Hope depends on our actions. If we don't do anything, there is little hope of changing the outcome.

Timing is key. You must act quickly. You must be willing to work on the issues in front of you if you are to create a hopeful situation. If you do nothing, you will incur the consequences and damage from your lack of action. In other words, you cannot just sit back and hope as you do nothing. You must engage and be part of the restoration process. Then you have the hope of restored relationships and mended connections.

The way you manage this process is more important than just getting through this time. How you relate to and interact with your children during crises determines the quality of your relationship with them in the future. How you stand with them during this difficult period determines the amount of time your children spend in darkness and the amount of damage they suffer and inflict on others as they struggle through their issues.

What I want you to understand is this: There is not much hope for parents who willingly sit back and do nothing when their children are struggling and in the process of destroying their lives. Those parents who become actively involved with their children during the struggle usually move on to have great relationships with their kids.

What If ...

The next question I often hear is, "What if my child never changes?"

That is a harder question to answer. Once in a while, even with all the efforts and intervention, a teen does not change. The way the child is now is the way he will be in twenty years. As much as I would like to tell you that every teen and family I ever met is doing well today, a few still struggle. Thankfully, the number of those in that category is small.

Where is the hope in this situation? There are some things you can never change. As painful as this may be to hear, believing has nothing to do with it. You can hope all you want and believe all you want, but it is not going to change anything. Hope comes as you change your dreams, your hopes, and your expectations of your child.

Many times, parents feel great relief when they finally embrace who their children really are. They let go. They release the frustration and aggravation they feel watching their children openly defy their expectations. They also carry with them the assurance they did everything they could. They do not have to suffer the pain of regret and shame, knowing they gave up on their child too soon.

If your child gets stuck in destructive behaviors that follow her into adulthood, I pray God will give you a new vision for your child and that will learn to love in ways you never have. Aim to give your "lost" children, whatever their age, a taste of God's loving and gracious character and a touch of His love. Release them and trust that God will welcome them into His arms and touch their hearts in a way only He can.

What You Can Hold Onto

You gain confidence as you engage in the process and do what you know to do. You get an understanding of why your child does what he does. You also develop a belief system, get your house in order, set boundaries, remain strong when you need to be strong, learn to be sensitive, allow pain to have its full effect, and deal with your own issues that play a part in your child's struggles. All of these help you grow no matter what choices your child makes.

Pray, engage with your child, and hope something will take root to move your child to maturity and responsibility. Pray you and your family will be able to restore healthy relationships for generations to come.

Do what you need to do. Take control of those things over which you have control. Then wait with anticipation. See what God can do!

Bentley

Bentley sat across from me at a local coffee shop and shared how he hated his parents. He was rebellious and did some pretty stupid things. Now he wanted to restore his relationship with them. When I asked him why, his answer was simple.

Bentley said, "I don't want to be one of those thirty-year-old guys who sits around and complains about his parents. I want to resolve things now."

I was astounded at his willingness to make some changes. He committed to change without my having to convince him he needed to change. Bentley was seeking help, looking for counsel, and starting to turn back to his parents. I wish all the young people I counseled over the years were so easy.

Hope came easily for Bentley's parents because they saw evidence of his desire to change. After twelve months, Bentley was back in control. His parents called it a year-long turnaround. By God's grace, Bentley straightened his life out.

Usually, total transformation takes longer. Most teens have to be taught they need to change. Then they have to be taught how to change. Once those are in place, the actual process of change begins.

Change takes time. When you go on a diet, all the pounds do not fall off overnight. When your teen goes on a "bad behavior" diet, the bad habits do not fall away overnight either. Be patient. Extend grace. Stand firm. Connect in relationship. Make good memories.

What you can hold onto in the midst of this change (sometimes for dear life) is that God has not abandoned you. When you feel abandoned by your teen, other family members, and friends, God is there. When you feel an overarching sense of loneliness as you walk through this dark time, God has not abandoned you. All the parents I know who experienced difficult times with their children learned new ways of understanding God. It's no wonder. They need new guidance, new information, new resources, and new thoughts about how to get through something they never experienced, something new and painful and difficult.

Parents at the beginning stages of difficulty with their children are often disgruntled, unhappy, and unsettled as they look for new ways to help their kids. If this is you, the challenges you now face demand new solutions. God is providing you the perfect opportunity to learn something new from Him.

You can also grab onto the fact that God will use this awful situation in your life to mold you and your child in ways you would have never thought possible. I have seen the worst of situations turn into something absolutely amazing. God uses everything. He collects your tears. He stops at nothing to weave our lives into something beautiful.

Jessica

Jessica's mother and brother were camping in Canada when a brown bear attacked her mother and began to maul her. Jessica's brother could be heard on videotape telling his mother not to move, to play dead and the bear would leave. It didn't.

At that moment, a park ranger ran up to the bear to try to distract it. With one swipe of the bear's paw, the ranger was decapitated. The brother tried to distract the bear, and he was attacked. Jessica's mother died. Her brother was critically injured. Jessica had to deal with her mother's absence and vivid mental images of the horrific way she died.

I met Jessica when she was sixteen and her life was spinning out of control due to the external circumstances that turned her family upside-down. While she was at Heartlight, she met the fellow she would later marry. Today, Jessica and her husband are the proud parents of a sweet little baby.

Did God orchestrate the bear attack so Jessica would one day meet this new fellow, get married, and have a baby that is a blessing to the whole family? No. Did He use every situation in Jessica's life to bring her to the point of restoration where she is today? Absolutely.

What Does Hope Feel Like?

If your teen gradually fell into a pattern of inappropriate behaviors, it will take some time to pull out of the nosedive. As I stated throughout this book, a change of the heart is not normally the immediate response to new rules and consequences. New habits are hard to build into a teen's life. New rules and policies need time to take hold. But they will. Just hang in there.

Your teens are going to act like teens. But even as teens, they really do want a relationship with you. No matter how much they desire freedom and independence, they would still rather have you as a parent than a friend.

God will honor your efforts. Don't give up. Don't give in. Do give your teens all they need at this juncture in their lives. If you feel miserable in the midst of the struggle you are going through, I guarantee your child feels worse. This is the time they need your presence, your guidance, and your heart. Give them freely, and trust God to create a beautiful masterpiece out of your the current mess.

"And we know that God causes all things to work together for good to those who love God, to those who are called according to *His* purpose." (Romans 8:28 NASB)

NOTES

Chapter 1—Hope Amidst the Conflict

1. "Chavaleh," from the musical *Fiddler on the Roof*. Words by Sheldon Harnick, Music by Jerry Bock Copyright ©1964 (Renewed) Mayerling Productions Ltd. Administered by R&H Music and Jerry Bock Enterprises for the United States and Alley Music Corporation, Trio Music Company, and Jerry Bock Enterprises outside of the United States. Used by permission. All rights reserved.
2. AlbertEinstein.com. Accessed August 12, 2016.
3. Ursula K. Le Guin, *The Left Hand of Darkness* (New York, NY: Ace Books, 1969, 2000), p. 220.
4. Rick Warren, *The Purpose-Driven Life* (Grand Rapids, Michigan: Zondervan, 2002), p. 17.

Chapter 5—The Problem of Performance-Based Relationships
Dan Allender, *How Children Raise Parents* (Colorado Springs: WaterBrook Press, 2003), p. 89.

Chapter 6—Why Does My Child Act This Way?
J.R.R. Tolkien, *The Fellowship of the Ring* (New York: Houghton Mifflin, 2004), p. 348.

John Armor, "'I Did It...Because I Could'—Bill Clinton Writes His Own Epitaph," *Free Republic*, June 26, 2004.

Chapter 7—The Importance of Pain
C.S. Lewis, *The Problem of Pain* (New York: HarperCollins, 2001), p. 91.

Chapter 8—Losses Behind Behavior
David Damico, *The Faces of Rage* (Colorado Springs: NavPress, 1992), p. 47.

Chapter 11—Setting Boundaries
Henry Cloud and John Townsend, *Boundaries* (Grand Rapids: Zondervan, 1992), p. 29.

Chapter 12—Allowing Your Child to Be in Control
Mark Twain, *A Tramp Abroad* (Whitefish, MT: Kessinger Publishing, 2004), p. 301.
Henry Cloud and John Townsend, *Boundaries* (Grand Rapids: Zondervan, 1992), p. 78.

Chapter 13—Building Maturity by Giving Responsibility
David Damico, *The Faces of* Rage (Colorado Springs: NavPress, 1992), p. 65.
Oscar Wilde, *Lady Windermere's Fan* (Mineola, NY: Dover Publications, 1998), p. 50.
James A. Belasco and Ralph C. Stayer, *Flight of the Buffalo* (New York: Warner Books, 1993), p. 312.
Andy Law, *Creative Company* (New York: John Wiley & Sons, Inc., 1999), p. 86.

ABOUT THE AUTHOR

*M*ark and Jan Gregston began their work with teens forty years ago, when Mark was a youth minister at First Methodist Church in Tulsa, Oklahoma. Their involvement with Young Life moved them to open their home to work with those who were struggling through family crises. During the 1980s, while living at Kanakuk Kamp in Branson, Missouri, Mark served as the area director for Young Life.

In 1989, Mark and Jan moved with their two children, Adam and Melissa, to Hallsville, Texas. Here they started Heartlight, a residential counseling center for struggling teens and families in crisis. To date, more than three thousand kids have resided in the Heartlight program, located in the beautiful piney woods of East Texas.

Believing that relationships create an arena for change, Mark and Jan share their lives through retreats, speaking engagements, counseling, national radio program *Parenting Today's Teens with Mark Gregston*, and the Heartlight Ministries residential program.

Mark travels most weekends, speaking or leading parenting seminars in cities across North America. He is also the proud grandfather of four: Maile (16), Macie (11), Chase (5), and Carter (3). For more information, visit www.HeartlightMinistries.org and www.ParentingTodaysTeens.org.

FAMILIES IN CRISIS
C O N F E R E N C E

A CONFERENCE FOR PARENTS IN CRISIS
HOSTED IN *TWO FORMATS.* **LED BY MARK GREGSTON,**
AMERICA'S LEADING EXPERT ON TEENS AND FAMILY.

OR

A **CONFERENCE** AT THE
HEARTLIGHT CAMPUS
IN LONGVIEW, TEXAS

AN **ONLINE CONFERENCE**
WITH **MARK GREGSTON**
LOCATED WHERE YOU ARE

TO RESERVE A SPOT OR FOR MORE
INFORMATION VISIT
WWW.**FAMILYCRISISRETREAT**.COM

TO RESERVE A SPOT OR FOR MORE
INFORMATION VISIT
WWW.**FICCZOOM**.COM

NOW AVAILABLE **IN PERSON** OR **ONLINE**

HEARTLIGHT

A RELATIONAL ATMOSPHERE
— COMMITTED TO **EXCELLENCE**

Since our humble beginning in 1988, Heartlight has become the country's premier residential counseling center and boarding school for struggling teens.

Located on 150 acres in the beautiful piney woods outside of Longview, Texas, Heartlight is a program that not only modifies behavior, but one that seeks to offer a unique, transformative experience through a relational experience that offers counseling, small group therapy, academics, and countless activities.

Heartlight's boutique approach creates a warm and welcoming atmosphere that offers hope to the hopeless, help to the discouraged, and new life to those who fear theirs would soon be lost. Parents are an integral part of the Heartlight experience. Their involvement through phone calls, participation at retreats, and commitment to having their child finish the program, all work together for a promising return home.

"Our daughter shared that she might not be alive had it not been for the work of Heartlight."

IN THEIR OWN WORDS

STORIES OF TROUBLED TEENS
a new video every week.

This new channel is unprecedened for Heartlight and Parenting Today's Teens. For the first time, this channel and all of its content is brought to you straight from the mouths and hearts of teens who reside at Heartlight.

In a "no holds barred" fashion, the good and downright ugly are discussed and seen by all viewers who watch the weekly videos on the channel.

The concentration of the stories will be the teens and having them talk... on their own terms...about their past, present, and future.

These videos act as a visual diagram of how the Heartlight program actually works and how these teenagers lives

change...right before your viewing eyes - creating a new episode each week.

You can choose to watch every Sunday (when it is posted) or binge watch at your leisure. Each video will only be 8 minutes long! And once on the channel, it stays there forever. Allowing you to re-watch or refer a friend. Unlike Netflix, SUBSCRIBING to our channel is FREE. No charge whatsoever. And by SUBSCRIBING, you will be notified with every new episode.

CRISIS COACHING PROGRAM

If you find yourself unable to find the right counsel to help you through a difficult situation with your teen, then our Crisis Coaching Program may be a resource that can help give you tools to avoid further conflict.

Our Families in Crisis Coaching Program gives parents the opportunity to speak directly with counseling professionals—also known as our Crisis Coaches. Over the phone, from wherever you're located, they'll assess your family's situation, coach you on how to get your family through the crisis, and offer proven parenting techniques.

IF YOU'RE IN A CRISIS, DON'T WAIT. HOPE AND HELP ARE JUST A PHONE CALL AWAY.

903.668.2173

WWW.HEARTLIGHTMINISTRIES.ORG/**PHONE-COUNSELING**

PARENTING RESOURCES

We are passionate about guiding kids and parents
through the turbulent teenage years. We've created these free online
resources as a way to offer effective and practical ways for parents to
counter the influence today's culture is having on their child.

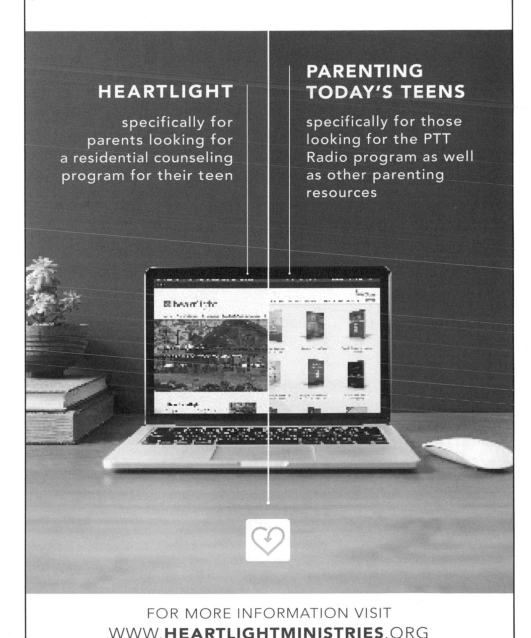

HEARTLIGHT

specifically for
parents looking for
a residential counseling
program for their teen

PARENTING TODAY'S TEENS

specifically for those
looking for the PTT
Radio program as well
as other parenting
resources

FOR MORE INFORMATION VISIT
WWW.**HEARTLIGHTMINISTRIES**.ORG